D1483018

DISCOVER CANADA

Prince Edward Island

By Deirdre Kessler

Consultants

Desmond Morton, FRSC, Professor of History, University of Toronto

Douglas Baldwin, History Department, Acadia University

Eldon Jamieson, Education Consultant, Charlottetown

Grolier Limited
TORONTO

Confederation Centre of the Arts, Charlottetown
Overleaf: **Boats and bait sheds near Stanhope**

Canadian Cataloguing in Publication Data

Kessler, Deirdre
    Prince Edward Island

(Discover Canada)
Rev. ed.
Includes index.
ISBN 0-7172-3137-2

1. Prince Edward Island — Juvenile literature.
I. Title. II. Series : Discover Canada (Toronto, Ont.)

FC2611.2.K48 1996   j971.7   C96-931026-9
F1047.4.K48 1996

Front cover: Cousin's Shore
Back cover: East Point Lighthouse in winter

Printed and bound in Canada.
Published simultaneously in the United States.
2 3 4 5 6 7 8 9 10   DWF   99 98 97 96

Springvale farm

Table of Contents

CHAPTER 1

Cradled on the Waves

One morning just a few years ago, Barb McNeill greased herself up and entered the water at Cape Tormentine, New Brunswick. Ignoring cold currents, waves and jellyfish, she swam and swam, crossing the paths of yellow perch and white-sided dolphins. Eleven hours and twenty-three minutes later, Barb's feet touched ground and she came ashore at Summerside, Prince Edward Island, her home town.

"It's very difficult to explain," she said, "but when I saw the lighthouse and Holman's Island, my heart was pounding with excitement. I love this place."

For thousands of years before Europeans found their way to North America, the Micmac people lived on the island. They called it *Minegoo* or *Abegweit*, which means "cradled on the waves." It was a place of plenty, where clams, oysters and mussels could be gathered easily from the shores. It was a place where strawberries, raspberries, blueberries and rosehips could be picked, where fish and waterfowl, deer, seals and beaver abounded.

Today, people whose ancestors came from many different countries love this place called Prince Edward Island. Perhaps they love it for its colour — its red clay, blue skies and bright green fields. Perhaps some love the Island because it is their native land or because it is so small it is possible to know almost everyone.

Many Islanders consider themselves to be at the heart of the world. This can be said of any home place, of course, but as you read through this book you may come to understand what it is in particular that Islanders so love about this piece of red clay.

The lighthouse at Seacow Head at the entrance to Bedeque Bay

CHAPTER 2
The Land

Prince Edward Island is Canada's smallest province, with an area of only 5660 square kilometres (2185 square miles). It is separated from Nova Scotia and New Brunswick on the south by the Northumberland Strait. To the north lies the Gulf of St. Lawrence, a relatively shallow valley of water which freezes in winter and warms quickly in summer.

Minegoo

The original settlers of Prince Edward Island, the Micmac, called it *Minegoo,* which simply means "the island." To this day, people who live in Prince Edward Island call their home "the Island," with a capital "I" as though it were the only island in the world.

There is a creation story about how Manitou, the Great Spirit of the Micmac people, had a portion of clay left over from the making of the earth and all things under the sun. He gave this clay to Glooscap, who formed it into a crescent and set it in the middle of the Laughing Waters, now known as the Gulf of St. Lawrence. Glooscap dipped his brush into the sunset and painted the land red, the colour of his people. He called it *Minegoo,* and every summer thereafter, he came to lie under the sheltering trees of its stately forests and listen to the whisperings of the wind and gentle waves.

Rolling Countryside and Rich Red Soil

One of most noticeable features about the Island is that it is, indeed, small. It is possible to drive from one end to the other of the

Overleaf: **Aerial view of the patchwork of fields and woodlots around New London**

The road into
Burlington

224-kilometre (140-mile) long, crescent-shaped land in half a day.
Because the Island is only 6 to 64 kilometres (4 to 40 miles) wide, it
is very easy to go back and forth from the north shore to the south.
At its narrowest point, a waist of land between Malpeque and
Bedeque bays, you can see from one shore to another.

There are no mountains on Prince Edward Island, but almost all
the land is gently rolling. The point of highest elevation at
Springton in Queens County is 139.5 metres (458 feet) above sea
level. Just under half of the province is forested, and the rest is
covered with a patchwork of working and abandoned farms and
fallow land. From the air, the Island looks very tidy with its patches
of forest and fields of grain, potatoes and hay.

Island soil is red because of the high amount of iron oxide in it.
In spring, when trees are just putting out their delicate green leaves
and fields are freshly ploughed for the new crops, the earth looks
especially red.

Origins

The Maritimes basin was formed about 300 million years ago, part of the Northern Appalachian Mountain belt. Several times during those millions of years, glaciers came to cover much of North America and then retreated.

Fifteen thousand years ago, during the last of these periods of glaciation, a three-kilometre (two-mile) thickness of ice still covered what is now Prince Edward Island. The weight of the ice had pushed the earth down. Then, as the ice melted, the crust of the earth floated up, and the Island began to rise above water.

Prince Edward Island reached its maximum land area about 7000 years ago. At that time it was connected to what are now New Brunswick and Nova Scotia by Northumbria, a land bridge. As the glacier continued to retreat northward, the melting ice caused the sea level to rise. By about 5000 years ago, it had risen enough to cover the land bridge, thereby creating an island.

The story of living things — plants and animals — on the Island can be read in the relatively soft shale and sandstone layers and mudstone that underlie the topsoil. We know, for instance that the Island was once a home to dinosaurs. In 1845, an archaeologist found the remains of a *Bathygnathus borealis* in a well in Cavendish. This small dinosaur was a flesh eater with a large sail on its back.

More recently, in layers of exposed rock along the shoreline, a geologist has found the footprints of ancient reptiles pursuing and being pursued.

Rivers and Lakes

The rivers and streams that flow from the interior of the Island meet with salt water at their mouths. Tides in both the Gulf of St. Lawrence and Northumberland Strait flow quite far up these streams, mixing the salt water of the ocean with fresh water. The Hillsborough River, the longest river on the Island, has its source not

Along the north shore of the Island, stark red cliffs rise in dramatic contrast to white sand beaches and dunes.

far from St. Peter's on the north shore and its mouth on the south shore, at Hillsborough Bay.

There are only a few small lakes in the province. These are fed by freshwater springs.

Climate

It is sometimes said that the Island's four seasons are early winter, winter, late winter and mud season. Like that of other Maritime provinces, the Island's climate is affected by the water that surrounds it. Both winter and summer are less severe in a maritime climate than in an inland one. Unlike parts of the other two Maritime provinces, Prince Edward Island does not have a fog season. Generally speaking, southwest winds blowing over water bring in warm, moist air which causes fog. But the southwest winds affecting the Island come off the land, and so they don't usually produce fog. Sometimes if there is a southwest flow of air for days on end, the Island will get fog from the Bay of Fundy and coastal Nova Scotia.

Winter begins early in December, but snow may fall during any of the autumn months. The mean January temperature is -7°C (19°F),

13

though the temperature has been known to drop to -28°C (-18°F). The average winter snowfall is about 330 centimetres (130 inches). When severe winter winds and snowstorms disrupt ferry service, Islanders say, "The mainland had been cut off," an expression that has its roots in the days when Prince Edward Island was self-sufficient.

The Strait of Northumberland and the Gulf of St. Lawrence freeze in January or February and remain frozen until the end of April. Spring is often short, with frequent temperature dips below freezing. But when summer arrives, there is no doubt as to why the Island is such a popular vacation place. Both the Northumberland Strait and the Gulf of St. Lawrence are warm enough for comfortable swimming in July and August. The mean July temperature is 18°C (64°F), with the highest temperature on record being 34.4°C (94°F). The average rainfall is about 840 millimetres (33 inches). Precipitation of some form falls on about 174 days of the year. The frost-free growing season is from about May 16 to October 14, though wise gardeners never plant tomatoes and other delicate crops until after June 10.

Autumn near Richmond, Prince County

The Wind

When a land mass gets hotter than the air over the water surrounding it, the hot air over the land rises, and cool air from the sea flows in. This uneven heating of the earth's surface gives rise to winds. At nighttime, the process reverses — the land becomes cooler than the water surrounding it, and so the air flow goes from land to sea. Alternating sea breezes and land breezes are a feature of Prince Edward Island which make windpower a realistic alternate energy source. Wind farms could one day be a good source of electricity for Islanders.

Plants

Prince Edward Island was once covered with tall hardwoods and white pine. When Britain used the Island as its shipyard in the first half of the nineteenth century, nearly every stand of beech, oak and white pine was felled for lumber. Virtually no original forest remains. Second-growth forests of coniferous trees now cover about 42 percent

Purple lupins

of the Island, with maple, white and yellow birch, and a few other hardwoods mixed in.

Spruce, alder and red maple grow on abandoned farmland. Hedgerows of chokecherry, wild rose, raspberries, tansy and Queen Anne's lace are common. Near the shore, blueberries, cranberries and bayberry plants mingle with thickets of wild roses and raspberry canes. Club mosses, marram grass and sedges grow thickly over the sand dunes.

In spring, the woods bloom with mayflowers, lady slipper orchids, pitcher plants and violets. Purple cow vetch, red and yellow paintbrush, daisies, clover and timothy grow in a typical summer hayfield. In some areas, wild lupins carpet the roadsides with blue, purple and pink flowers.

Animals

In the past 500 years, humans have greatly changed the patterns of animal life on Prince Edward Island and in its surrounding sea. Once there were great auks. Passenger pigeons were so thick in the air at times that the sun was blotted out. Once there were large mammals — caribou, bear, moose, bobcat and cougar. Now the largest undomesticated land animals are beaver, fox, snowshoe hare, raccoon and skunk.

There are harbour and grey seals in the waters surrounding the Island. In spring, harp seals give birth on the ice of the Gulf of St. Lawrence. The all-white baby seals have become an attraction. Helicopters bring visitors to the ice floes, adding a new source of income for tourist operators.

White-sided dolphins, sperm whales, Minke whales and occasionally humpback whales may be seen in Island waters. In some years there are quite a few instances of whales and dolphins swimming into shallow water and being unable to get back to sea. Sickness or electrical storms may drive them onto a beach, or they may simply go too close to the shore chasing food. The P.E.I.

Left: **Harp seal mother and pup.** *Right:* **Colony of cormorants at Cape Tryon on the north shore**

Stranding Network has a team of trained volunteers to help stranded animals back to sea or to care for them until they can be returned to their natural environment.

In the past decade or so, coyotes have moved to the Island, probably crossing over the ice on the Northumberland Strait in winter. They are not popular with farmers as they worry and sometimes kill livestock.

There are no poisonous snakes and only a few species of reptiles and amphibians on the Island.

Three hundred species of birds live on or pass through Prince Edward Island. In addition to the provincial bird, the blue jay, year-round residents include black-capped chickadee, crow, ruffed grouse and barred owl. Waterfowl, including the Canada goose, brant, black and ring-necked ducks, and many other migratory birds live in marshes and bays. Great blue herons feed in shallow water and nest in the tops of spruce trees. Marsh hawks cruise the up- and down-drafts by shoreline dunes. A story is told of a saw-whet owl driven by severe winter weather to capture and devour a starling on Main Street in Montague.

Cultured mussels, clams, oysters, salmon, trout, mackerel, hake and many other species of fish and shellfish can be found in Prince Edward Island waters. Lobster was once so plentiful in Island waters that it was used as a fertilizer.

CHAPTER 3
The People

There are six sites on Prince Edward Island that point to the arrival of people, the proto-Micmac, during the time of the land bridge. (Proto means "first in time.") Archaeologists believe proto-Micmac people roamed the land hunting the caribou as their main source of food. They also hunted other animals, including large sea mammals, and gathered edible plants and roots.

Some of the tools these people used for hunting seal, whales and walrus have been found in Maritime waters. A 6500-year-old *ulu* — a kind of knife used to butcher walrus and whales — was found a few years ago in the Gulf of St. Lawrence. The Inuit in Canada's North still use a similar knife today when they hunt.

Copper beads, quartzite cobbles and slate-etched designs on tools and decorative items have been found on the north shore of the Island. These items are linked to cultures based far from the Maritimes and are evidence of the movement of different peoples in and out of the area. The early traders who brought them would have travelled across Northumbria, the land bridge that once existed between the Island and the mainland.

Micmac

Archaeologists have found pottery and piles of shells 2000 to 3000 years old on Prince Edward Island's north shore. These discoveries indicate that a new people, the Micmac, were permanent residents.

The Micmac's lives were based on the seasons. In summer, they gathered oysters and clams, and fished for mackerel, halibut and cod. They collected strawberries, raspberries and blueberries, gathered nuts and wild peas, and hunted for mammals, birds and

Top: Aspects of Micmac life are illustrated at the Micmac Indian Village at Rocky Point. *Above left:* Playground at John J. Sark Memorial School at Lennox Island. *Above right:* Mural by Lennox Island artist Michael Francis, showing Glooscap carrying Prince Edward Island from heaven to Malpeque Bay to share with his favourite people, the Micmac

bird's eggs. They wove baskets of all sizes and shapes — small ones for berry picking, large ones for storage of roots and many other items. They made other containers from birch bark and moose hide, and wove mats of reeds and grass to cover their wigwams.

In the fall and winter, other mammals were hunted, such as moose, caribou, bear and beaver. Salmon, eels and trout caught in the autumn were smoked for winter use. Rabbit, deer, seal and walrus could be hunted when snow covered the ground.

In spring, the Micmac collected maple sap and made syrup. Greens and shoots and fresh seafood were again added to the diet.

Each Micmac village had its elders whose advice was valued regarding important aspects of village life, hunting boundaries, alliances with other communities and trade excursions to the Bay of Fundy or New England for stone and corn. Everyone co-operated in making canoes, building new wigwams and making basket traps and weirs to catch migrating fish.

Micmac planned large feasts and invited neighbouring villages to participate in games, storytelling, drumming and dancing. These gatherings were usually held in the summer and lasted several days. Often it was during this time that young people were able to meet future mates.

Storytellers were much honoured by the Micmac. Stories guided spiritual and practical life. Stories framed the entire culture of the Micmac — who they were, where they came from, the great deeds of individuals, the traits of animals, medicinal uses of plants.

Several thousand Micmac were living on the Island when the first Europeans arrived. The Europeans came in vessels larger than the Native people had ever seen, bringing with them gifts of metal and cloth. They also brought an entirely different attitude towards life. Over time, the Europeans forced the Micmac to change their lifestyle, and the diseases they brought with them led to the death of many. By 1880 the Native population had fallen to 266. Today, there are about 1500 Micmac on Prince Edward Island, about 600 of whom live on four reserves at Lennox Island, Rocky Point, Scotchfort and Morell.

The Basques

The Basques were noted sailors and fishing people who came to Prince Edward Island during the 1600s. Their home was in the Pyrenees, mountains that separate France and Spain. Archae-ologists have found the skeletal remains of seven Basque sailors, and the story of a Basque girl named La Belle Marie is still part of the oral tradition of Island Micmac. There are at least ten written versions of this legend of a Basque girl who marries the son of a Micmac chief. In some versions, Marie lives happily ever after. In others, either she or her husband is shot and killed. In still another account of the story, Marie was brought to trial, condemned and executed for witchcraft. The burning supposedly took place on November 17, 1723, at Port LaJoye, across the harbour from present-day Charlottetown.

The French and Acadia

Jacques Cartier made three voyages to North America for the King of France. On his first voyage in 1534, he landed on the Island and described it in his diary as "the fairest land 'tis possible to see."

It was not until 1604, however, that the French first tried to establish a colony in the area that would become known as Acadia, on the east coast of North America. It was almost 30 years more before permanent settlement really began. In 1632 a group of 300 colonists arrived at La Hève, in modern-day Nova Scotia. These people were the ancestors of most of the Acadians who now live in Nova Scotia, New Brunswick, Prince Edward Island, Quebec and Louisiana.

By 1700, there were more than 1000 Acadians living in the region now known as the Maritimes. They worked hard draining swamps and marshland. They established closely-knit communities in which neighbours helped one another build houses and barns, cut wood, harvest marsh hay and build dykes.

The area of major settlement by the Acadians on Île St-Jean — as the Island was then named — was at St-Pierre, with a few pioneering families at Port LaJoye, Trois Rivières and Souris. Throughout those first difficult years of settlement, an even more difficult period of persecution, and into the present day, Acadians have been a strong presence in Prince Edward Island.

Today, there are about 10 000 people of Acadian descent in the province. Acadian cultural centres in Mont-Carmel, Miscouche,

Celebrating Acadian heritage at the Mont-Carmel Acadian Village

Charlottetown and North Rustico ensure the preservation of the Acadian heritage and revitalization of the language and culture. Francophone schools and French immersion classes in the province are thriving. Acadian music, theatre, literature, dance, crafts and other cultural expressions flourish. Yearly festivals and on-going cultural organizations such as the Saint Thomas Aquinas Society keep Acadian culture and traditions alive.

The British

When most of North America became British territory in 1763, Île St-Jean was renamed St. John's Island. New settlers — English, Scottish and Irish — began to arrive. The population of the Island grew from a few hundred Micmac and Acadians to 7000 people by 1805, and by 1881, 109 000 people were living in the province, most of them of British origin. Today, the majority of Island residents are of British descent, and it is the British culture and system of government and the English language which have been the most influential forces in the shaping of the province.

Americans

When the American Revolution (1775-1783) ended, about 600 Loyalists — people who chose to remain loyal to Great Britain — left the newly created United States to settle the British territory of St. John's Island. Many of these people did not stay because they could not buy land, but only rent it from landlords.

Most of the migration between the Island and the United States in the late nineteenth and early twentieth century was the other way — with Islanders going to "the Boston States" in New England to find work. A solid connection between New England and the Island was built during this period, and today there are many Islanders who either were born in the United States or have relatives there.

Blacks

In the 1780s, some of the Loyalists who escaped to Canada brought their Black slaves with them. A number of free Blacks came as well, many of them men who had won their freedom by fighting for Britain during the Revolution and later during the War of 1812. Runaway slaves also made their way to Prince Edward Island.

Truckman in the Bog district of Charlottetown about 1895

There was never really a separate Black community on the Island as there was in Nova Scotia. In a poor, racially mixed section of Charlottetown called The Bog, the Black population, numbering about a hundred, flourished from around 1810 until 1900. At no time did the number of Blacks province-wide exceed 200, and over time, they were assimilated into the larger Island population.

Lebanese

In the late 1800s and early 1900s, there was a great emigration of people from Lebanon. They established communities in many parts of the world, including Prince Edward Island. Many of those who settled in the province became traders or pack peddlers who travelled from farm to farm selling housewares, tea, clothing and tools. Often when they had saved enough money, they opened corner stores, many of which still exist today. The success of Lebanese merchants led them to other commercial enterprises, and they became an important part of the province's social, cultural and political life. Prominent among them is Joe Ghiz, who became premier of Prince Edward Island in 1986.

Other Twentieth-century Immigrants

A shortage of farming land in the Netherlands brought many Dutch immigrants to Prince Edward Island, with the largest influx just after the Second World War.

Guatamalans, Salvadoreans, East Indians, Chinese, Germans and others from every continent and many countries of the world have immigrated to Prince Edward Island, bringing with them their diverse languages and customs. These people have enriched Island life and created a multicultural community which has added greatly to Island culture and tradition.

CHAPTER 4
Colonial Struggles

After Jacques Cartier's visits to North America, more Frenchman and other Europeans came, attracted by the abundance of fur-bearing animals and fish, especially cod. At first, there was no thought of settling permanently in this "new" land. The Europeans traded for furs with the Native people, caught and dried cod, and then took what they had gathered back to Europe.

The Acadian Period

Eventually, in the early 1600s, the wealth of natural resources on land and in the sea led France to establish a colony in North America. A French nobleman, Pierre du Gua de Monts, was given the right to fish and trade in the region now called the Maritime Provinces. In return, de Monts was to bring settlers to the area.

After several setbacks, a French colony finally took hold in the 1630s. The early settlers called their home l'*Acadie,* or Acadia, a name that may have come from the Micmac word *quoddy* or *cady,* meaning "a pleasant piece of land."

The Acadians cleared patches of forest, dyked and drained swamps and marshland, put up log homes, storehouses and animal shelters, and struggled to survive the hardships of winter. Soon, however, they found themselves involved in another sort of struggle.

Both Britain and France wanted control of Acadia for its strategic location. France had established a colony, New France, along the St. Lawrence River and needed control of the waterway for easy access

View of Charlottetown about 1832

Interior of an Acadian house

to it. The British controlled lands to the north — on Hudson Bay — and to the south in the Thirteen Colonies. They wanted to ensure that France could not attack them from Acadia.

Throughout the seventeenth century, Acadia was a battleground between Britain and France. Meanwhile, the Acadians felt no particular loyalty to either of these countries. They were loyal only to their own small communities, and to the fields they had worked so hard to clear, plant and harvest.

In 1713, France lost a war with Britain for North America, and so most of Acadia — present-day New Brunswick and mainland Nova Scotia — was granted to Great Britain. France was left in possession of Île Royale, Île St-Jean and New France — present-day Cape Breton, Prince Edward Island and Quebec.

In 1719, the King of France gave Île St-Jean to the Comte de Saint-Pierre on condition that he settle it with Roman Catholics. The following summer, about 250 colonists sailed into the Hillsborough Harbour and landed at Port LaJoye, which became the capital of the colony. About the same time, France began to build the Fortress of Louisbourg on the tip of Île Royale in order to control access to the St. Lawrence River.

The colonists who came to Île St-Jean brought animals, grain and tools. Within a few years, tiny settlements dotted the coast and the banks of the Hillsborough River. In the patches of ground they cleared around their log houses, the new settlers planted cabbages, turnips, peas and wheat. They cleared giant timbers and pulled stubborn stumps from the earth to make fields. They fished the bountiful sea, and slowly built up their stock of cattle, pigs and horses. A portion of all that was grown or raised was collected and shipped to the soldiers at Louisbourg.

In 1745, the British captured the fortress at Louisbourg. Some of the British fleet then sailed to Île St-Jean and destroyed the settlements at Port LaJoye and Trois Rivières. A small band of Micmac joined forces with the Port LaJoye soldiers, who had fled up the Hillsborough River, and together they drove the invaders back to their vessels.

Peace talks in 1748 gave Louisbourg back to France. The British then tried to extract a promise from the Acadians living in Nova Scotia that they would fight against France in any future conflicts. Most refused, and although no harm came to them, many Acadians decided to move to Île St-Jean. By 1751, the Acadian population on the Island had more than doubled.

The Deportation

In 1755, the British governor of Nova Scotia again demanded that the Acadians in the colony sign an oath of loyalty that required them to fight for the British. This time when most still refused to sign, the governor ordered that they all be deported to other British colonies. About 2000 Acadians escaped to Île St-Jean as 10 000 others were rounded up and sent into exile.

The following year, war again broke out between Britain and France. When the British captured the French fortress at Louisbourg in 1758, war ships under command of Lord Rollo sailed to Île St-Jean to claim the Island for Britain. Lord Rollo's orders were to destroy all crops and livestock, deport all Acadians and build a fort.

The deportation of Island Acadians. Of the 3500 Acadians who were sent into exile in 1758, 700 were drowned when some of the ships carrying them across the Atlantic sank in a storm.

Many Island Acadians escaped Lord Rollo's men with help from the Micmac. Some went to New France or fled to the French islands of Saint-Pierre and Miquelon; a few hid out in the woods. Eventually, the British rounded up 3500 Acadians and sent them to Louisbourg, and from there to France. Most of the Island's present-day Acadian population is descended from the families who managed to escape the deportation or those who later returned.

The Micmac During the Acadian Period

The climate and geography of France and Île St-Jean were different enough to cause severe problems for the early French settlers. The Micmac generously helped the newcomers, showing them what was safe to eat, where favourable sites were for shelters, how to make and use moccasins, snowshoes, toboggans and canoes, and how to hunt and fish. Many Acadians would have starved had they not been given food by the Micmac people.

In a very short time, however, the Micmac's ancient way of life changed. They traded furs to the French for cloth, iron axes, knives and guns. Brandy, a new substance to Native people, became a trade item and further broke down the traditional way of life. Within a few decades, Acadians outnumbered Micmac and the dependency had shifted direction — the Micmac now relied on the Acadians for their food and clothing.

One of the worst things Europeans brought to the new land was disease. Influenza, smallpox, measles were unknown in North America and Native people had built up no immunity to them, as the Europeans had. A great many Micmac, along with Native people all over North America, died of these diseases.

Since people at that time had no knowledge of germs, the only explanation the Micmac had for these disastrous diseases and the deaths they caused was that something was wrong with their spiritual world. When their own healers and spiritual leaders proved powerless against the plagues, the harmony that existed in the Micmac world crumbled. Doubt and disorder filled their lives, and it became relatively easy for French missionaries to convert them to Roman Catholicism.

Landlords and Settlement

After Britain won the war against France, the Island's name was changed to St. John's Island, and King George III hired a man named Samuel Holland to survey the land.

Holland selected the location for the capital, Charlottetown, because it lay near the middle of the colony and had three rivers which could provide easy travel into the interior. Then he and his survey team divided the Island into 67 townships, or lots, of about 8000 hectares (20 000 acres) each. On July 23, 1767, most of these lots were given away by lottery to British citizens to whom the British government owed favours.

In return for the land, the new owners promised to bring in Protestant settlers and to pay an annual quitrent (or fee) to the government. Land that had already been cleared by the Acadians was the first to be claimed by the new British landlords. Many Acadian families moved to the more remote areas of the Island, to places such

Right: Island painter A.L. Morrison's portrayal of the lottery held in London in 1767 to distribute the Island lots to influential British citizens. *Below:* This map shows how Samuel Holland and his surveying team divided up the Island in 1764.

as Mont-Carmel, Miscouche, Bloomfield, Cascumpec, Egmont Bay, Tignish and Rollo Bay.

Most of the landlords did not live up to their end of the agreement. Within a decade about a quarter of them had sold their lots on the Island. But some landlords, including the surveyor Samuel Holland, did colonize the land. From 1770 to 1775, about 1000 settlers from England and Scotland came to the Island. John MacDonald, Laird of Glenaladale, brought 214 mainly Roman Catholic Scottish Highlanders to Tracadie in 1772. In 1784, about 600 Loyalists arrived following the American Revolution. In 1803, Thomas Douglas, Earl of Selkirk, brought 800 Highland Scots to land in the Orwell-Point Prim area of the Island.

Few of the early British settlers were prepared for the harsh life that awaited them. There was still a great deal of forested land to clear. Winters were long and bitterly cold compared to those at home. Promised shipments of food, farm equipment and horses sometimes did not reach the Island.

Still the settlers made headway, clearing forestland, planting crops, building mills, houses and barns. By 1805, the population of the Island had grown to about 7000, and by 1820 there were 15 000 people living in villages along the coast.

Between 1810 and 1835, about 3000 Irish immigrants came to the Island. The potato famines in Ireland brought another 4000 in the 1840s, and by 1848 there were 6763 Irish-born settlers living on Prince Edward Island. Scottish immigrants from the Hebrides, Western Highlands, Argyle and Skye continued to settle the Island for a hundred years after the Great Land Lottery of 1767.

Early Government on the Island

In 1770, the government of Great Britain sent an Irishman, Captain Walter Patterson, to govern St. John's Island. In 1773, the first elections were held. The 18 men elected formed the Legislative Assembly, a body that drew up laws. However, the governor was not bound to carry out the Assembly's wishes, and no bill could become law without his approval. Moreover, the government of Great Britain could disallow any bill within two years of its being passed by the Island Assembly.

Walter Patterson governed St. John's Island for 16 years. Largely thanks to his efforts, the colony grew from about 300 people to a population 5000 during this period. But Patterson cheated the public by holding a secret auction of land and buying 40 000 hectares (100 000 acres) for himself for a small sum. He was dismissed as a result, and when he finally returned to Britain in 1789, he was bankrupt and lived in poverty for the rest of his life.

In 1799, the Island had its last name change: it became Prince Edward Island in honour of the son of King George III.

A Question of Land

For over a hundred years, settlers on the Island were frustrated because they were not able to buy the land they worked so hard to farm. The landlords collected rents, increased them as they pleased, and sometimes evicted settlers who did not pay on time. Many landlords never left Britain. They hired agents to live on the Island and collect rents. Tenant farmers hated most agents.

William Cooper was an agent for British landlord Lord Townshend. He settled near Bay Fortune, built ships, put up a mill, farmed and collected rent from Townshend's tenants. Then, in 1829, Townshend fired him. Cooper quickly switched sides and became a supporter of the tenant farmers. When voters elected him to the Assembly in 1831, he organized a political party that worked to help tenants buy the land they farmed. He encouraged tenants to refuse to pay their rents, and as a result, many tenants were arrested or thrown off their land. Secretly, however, Cooper had continued to pay his own rent and so he was able to keep his farm. When the tenants learned of this, they rejected him, although they still supported his ideas about land reform.

Opposition to the landlords continued to grow, and reformers gradually took control of the Assembly. It became clear, however, that they would get nowhere as long as the governor and his influential advisors could ignore the majority members of the Assembly. Reformers on the Island, like those in Nova Scotia and elsewhere, began to demand responsible government. In a responsible government, the advisors of the governor would have to have the support of the majority of members in the Assembly. If the government leaders lost the support of the Assembly, they would have to resign.

In 1851, three years after the example was set in Nova Scotia, Prince Edward Islanders achieved responsible government. George Coles became government leader, or premier, and in 1853, he and his supporters passed the Land Purchase Act. Under this bill, if a landlord was willing to sell, the government could buy any estate over 400 hectares (1000 acres) and then sell the land to the tenants. The Land Purchase Act met with limited success — in 20 years, tenant farmers were able to buy nearly a quarter of the Island. But landlords could still refuse to sell, and the strife did not stop until Confederation in 1873.

The Age of Sail

A glance at a map of Prince Edward Island will explain one reason why the shipbuilding industry thrived. There are hundreds of sheltered harbours all along its coastline, perfect settings for building and launching vessels. As well, the Island was covered with magnificent trees: white pine for spars and masts, juniper and spruce for planking, and oak and beech for keels and masts.

About 4500 sailing vessels were built on the Island during the period from 1820 to 1880. The sailing industry generated work for shipwrights, merchants, blacksmiths, sailmakers and many other craftspeople. In shipyards on nearly every bay and river, workers

Charlottetown Harbour in the 1820s

built schooners, brigantines, brigs, barques and barquentines. By 1850, the Island was self-sufficient and prosperous. The era is often referred to as "the golden age."

Island-built ships sailing to Great Britain carried cargoes of squared timber which were sold at a good profit to ship owners. Two communities with especially fine harbours, Summerside and Georgetown, prospered greatly, and many other communities had thriving shipbuilding centres. A group of merchants grew powerful during the age of sail, including the Macdonalds of Cardigan, the Popes of Summerside, the Duncans and Peakes of Charlottetown, and the Yeo family of Port Hill.

The golden era of shipbuilding came to a close when all of the best trees had been cut down. As well, after 1875, steam ships built with steel replaced sailing vessels. It was during this post-sail age that many Islanders left to find work in New England.

Farming and Fishing

Overlapping the golden age of sail was a similar era of prosperity in farming and fishing. With the groundwork done by the Acadian and British pioneers, farmers during the period from 1850 to 1880 were able to grow many crops successfully. This period was also a time when new agricultural methods, such as crop rotation and the use of fertilizers, improved the productivity on nearly every family farm. Grain and potatoes grew especially well in the Island's loamy soil, and pastureland was lush. Crops and livestock were so successful that oats, potatoes and pork were exported to Great Britain, Newfoundland and the other Maritime provinces.

Cod was an enormously rich fishery resource. Cod oil, salt cod, dried cod, cod cheeks and cod tongues were sold to the United States along with other fish such as mackerel, gaspereau and herring. Oyster fishing in the Island's many bays also became a profitable business. Lobster, once so plentiful that farmers dumped tonnes of it on their fields as fertilizer, became popular as a table food.

The Micmac during the British Period

The British were not as friendly with the Micmac as the Acadians had been, and did not permit them to roam the Island freely. When the Micmac asked for land, the government refused. One British landlord, Sir James Montgomery, offered Lennox Island rent-free to the Micmac, and a few families went to live year-round on that relatively infertile island in Malpeque Bay. The remaining several hundred Micmac continued to hunt and fish as best they could. They also travelled the countryside peddling baskets, quillwork, brooms, snowshoes, canoes and other handcrafted items.

In 1832, Micmac elders petitioned government leaders for land for their people. They gently reminded them of promises made and not kept, and pointed out that the Micmac in other provinces had been given land. Their petition fell on deaf ears. It was not until 1870 that a British charitable group bought Lennox Island for the Micmac. The British considered the idea of establishing reserves, specific areas set aside where Native people would live separate from people of European descent. But when the Island joined Confederation in 1873, the Micmac were put under the control of the federal government. Still nothing changed for the Island's Native people.

Micmac camp, probably on Lennox Island

CHAPTER 5
Confederation to Modern Times

During the 1850s and 1860s, the British colonies in North America were still isolated from each other. For a variety of reasons, a movement to unite some of the colonies began, and in 1864 Nova Scotia and New Brunswick proposed a meeting on the Island to discuss a Maritime union. Government leaders from the United Province of Canada (now Ontario and Quebec) asked if they could come too.

At that time, Islanders were not very interested in a union either with other Maritime provinces or with the United Province. The hard work of farmers and fishermen was paying off, shipbuilding was thriving. The colony was self-sufficient and quite satisfied with things as they were.

The delegates to the now-famous Charlottetown Conference arrived on the Island to find the city filled with people who had come to see a circus. The Slaymaker & Nichols' Olympic Circus, complete with acrobats, equestrians, dogs, monkeys and a band, was the first circus to come to the Island in 21 years. All the hotels were filled. The delegates to the Conference had to return to sleep on board their steamer, the *Queen Victoria*.

On July 1, 1867, Confederation was achieved, with New Brunswick, Nova Scotia, Ontario and Quebec the first partners in the new relationship. The Island turned down requests to join until Sir John A. Macdonald, the prime minister of Canada, made the right offer at the right time.

In 1871, the Island began to build a railway and the cost quickly threatened to bankrupt the government. The Railway Act passed by

A recreation of the famous Robert Harris painting of the Fathers of Confederation. The original, which hung in the Parliament Building in Ottawa, was destroyed by fire in 1916.

the government set a limit on the cost per mile, but none on actual mileage. Because of this, the contractors who built the railway avoided hills and estuaries to keep the cost per mile below the fixed rate. Like a snake, the P.E.I. Railway curved through the Island countryside. Each mile cost no more than the agreed-upon sum, but the total cost of such a winding line got out of hand. The P.E.I. Railway cost eight times what it was expected to, and the Island government was bound by law to pay the bill.

In exchange for Prince Edward Island joining Confederation, Prime Minister Macdonald offered enough money to pay off the railway debts and to buy all the land owned by absentee landlords. As well, the Island was promised six, instead of the originally proposed five, members in the House of Commons in Ottawa and a continuous communication link with the mainland through the ferry service.

On July 1, 1873, Prince Edward Island became Canada's seventh province. Islanders accepted their fate without much enthusiasm. Here's how *The Charlottetown Patriot* described the inauguration ceremony:

> ...A few moments before 12, Mr. Sheriff Watson stepped forward on the balcony of the Colonial Building and read the Union Proclamation. He was accompanied by two ladies and about half a dozen gentlemen. The audience within hearing consisted of three persons, and even they did not appear to be very attentive. After the reading of the Proclamation was concluded, the gentlemen on the balcony gave a cheer, but the three persons below — who...at that moment represented the people of Prince Edward Island —responded never a word.

Getting to and from the Mainland

Crossing Northumberland Strait to the mainland in summer was never a problem. For centuries the Micmac canoed back and forth. Later, sailing vessels crossed fairly regularly, and in the 1860s, there was regular steamer service. Winter was a different matter. Between 1827 and 1918 small iceboats were used to carry mail and people

across. These iceboats could be rowed or sailed in ice-free lanes of water, or dragged across the ice by long leather straps by the crew. On a good day, a winter journey across the thick ice could take three or four hours. When the masses of ice drifted and built into five-metre-high (15-foot) ridges, or suddenly opened up revealing frigid black water, a crossing might take an entire day.

In keeping with its Confederation promise, Ottawa began a ferry service to the Island in 1875. Steamships crossed from Borden to Cape Tormentine on the New Brunswick shore. In 1918 a ferry capable of carrying automobiles and railway cars began service. For 70 years many different vessels with ice-breaking capabilities crossed the Strait every hour or so. In 1995, construction began on a fixed link to the mainland. This bridge is scheduled to open in 1997.

Northumberland Ferries Inc., a private company, runs a second ferry service between Wood Islands on the southeast coast and Caribou, Nova Scotia, during months when the Strait is ice-free.

The Railway

In the early 1990s, salvage workers tore up the railway ties and tracks that crossed Prince Edward Island, and the railway era came to what many considered a sad end. For almost a century, the railway had been a common thread through the fabric of Canada.

The Canadian dream of a transcontinental railway from coast to coast was echoed in Islanders' dreams when the Island's own railway project began in 1871. When it was completed, the Prince Edward Island Railway ran from Alberton at the western end of the Island to Georgetown at the eastern end, with branch lines to Souris and Tignish.

Islanders from all walks of life — farming and fishing people, traders and villagers — were enormously excited. They now had an easier way to transport their crops and livestock to markets. The Island's clay roads — the first road was not paved until 1934 —were seas of red mud in autumn and spring. Many outlying farms were inaccessible for several weeks of the year during these mud seasons.

Nearly every village demanded a branch line and station. This was a great boon to Islanders living outside Charlottetown or Summerside who wanted to go to town more than once a month. Many Island students took the train to and from high school. The 470 one-room rural schools went only to grade 10 and, until the 1930s, Charlottetown had the only school for grades 11 and 12 on the Island.

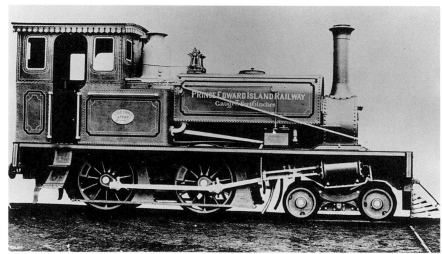

An early wood-fuelled engine of the Prince Edward Island Railway

Horses and Automobiles

For a long time, horses were the main mode of transportation on the Island, and they provided the power for most of the heavy work on farms and in the woods. Horses were also friends, often part of the family. Islanders' love of horses continues, and there are more horses on the Island in relation to the human population than in any other province in Canada. In recent years, a number of farmers have even returned to using horses to cultivate the land.

Harness racing is an industry and a pastime on the Island. In 1991, just over $6 million was bet at the Charlottetown Driving Park and the Summerside Raceway.

While Islanders retained their love of horses, they also adopted the automobile, though somewhat reluctantly. The first horseless carriage operated in Canada belonged to Father Georges-Antoine Belcourt, who drove his primitive automobile to a community picnic in

Horse-drawn buggies remained a common sight on rural roads long after Islanders accepted the inevitable and lifted their ban on automobiles.

Rustico in 1866. That event did not start a mad craze for cars, though it did drive a few horses crazy. There were only seven cars in Prince Edward Island in 1907.

In 1908, automobiles were actually banned from the Island, with a fine of $500 or a sentence of six months in jail going to any offender. The ban lasted until 1913, when it was changed to allow people to operate cars on certain roads on certain days. At that time there was a grand total of 26 cars on the Island. Anyone caught driving on Sunday, Tuesday, Friday or Saturday was fined. In 1918 the law was changed again to permit automobiles free access to Island roads.

Communications

In 1887, when Charlottetown got its first electric street lights, there were 11 telephones on the Island. In those times, news travelled by word of mouth and through the printed word in monthly, weekly and a few daily newspapers. Each village had a post office or general store that was its information centre.

The early days of radio on the Island are associated with one person, Keith S. Rogers, who nurtured a boyhood fascination with telegraphy into a career as the Island's first broadcaster. Rogers built and ran a radio station, CHCK, which operated from 1928 until the Second World War. He also planned the Island's first television station. His son-in-law, R.F. Large, broadcast the first television program on Prince Edward Island in 1956.

Today, Prince Edward Island has three AM and two FM stations, including one operated by the Canadian Broadcasting Corporation (CBC). CBAF-FM, a French-language station, originates in Moncton. The only television network producing programs is the CBC. The Canadian Television Network, CTV, transmits to the Island via a repeater station in Moncton. Cablevision and pay TV are available in the most populated areas. In remoter areas, many people have set up satellite dishes.

44

Air Travel

Air links between Prince Edward Island and the rest of the world began in 1941, when Carl Frederick Burke founded Maritime Central Airways. For more than 20 years Burke continued his air service before selling the company to Eastern Provincial Airways. Later, two major Canadian airlines brought service to the province, and, in 1992, a U.S. airline joined the market.

Commerce and Industry

In 1871, there were more than 500 mills of one kind or another on the Island. Shingle, sawlogs, grist (flour), woolcarding and clothfulling and dressing mills dotted the province. Small factories across the Island manufactured clothing, furniture, shoes, leather,

Left: Woollen Mill at North Tryon.
Below: Market day in Charlottetown. The Round Market seen here, with Province House behind it, was destroyed by fire in the 1860s.

sleighs, buggies and wheels, pottery, bricks, ploughs, potato hillers and mowing machines. People on the Island were able to produce just about everything they needed to make life comfortable. During these self-sufficient times before the turn of the twentieth century, Island entrepreneurs built their businesses with such success that many of the original companies still operate in the province today.

Beginning early in the nineteenth century, a large farmers' market in Charlottetown brought people from the countryside on Wednesdays and Saturdays to buy and sell butter, eggs, poultry, fish, meat, vegetables, oats, hay and wood. The first Charlottetown markets were built where Province House and the Confederation Centre of the Arts now stand. When the W.C. Harris Market burned in 1958, the tradition of having markets in the centre of town ended. In 1984, a new farmers' market was built at the edge of the city near the university.

Fox Farming

One local industry that boomed for a short while was silver fox farming. Until the 1890s, the rare black fox with its silver-tipped guard hairs was an occasional prize for trappers and hunters. Then,

The Fox Hall of Fame in Summerside presents the history of fox farming, which at one time represented 17 percent of the Island's economic base.

after years of experiments with the breeding of captive foxes, Robert Oulton and Charles Dalton succeeded in producing foxes with the desired silver pelts. They sold one of their fox pelts in England in 1900 for the then-fantastic price of $1800, and a few years later sold four fox pups locally for $10 000. The two soon made a fortune with their furs, but within a few years, the secret of their breeding techniques leaked out. The number of fox breeders on the Island grew to 300, and for a time, the industry was valued at about $20 million. The fox fur industry declined during the Second World War, and in 1986, there were only ten fox ranches left in the province. The practice of breeding foxes in captivity continues, however, and there is still an annual fox show and sale of live animals.

The First World War

When Britain declared war on Germany in August 1914, Canada was automatically at war as well. Many young Island men enlisted in the armed forces, and many died in battle. The community of St. Peter's was especially hard-hit, with scarcely a family that did not lose a son, brother, father or uncle in the war. Of a population of 64 male Micmacs from Lennox Island, 32 enlisted. Seven of them died on the battlefields in Europe. There were Islanders among the women who served as nurses overseas, and at home, women and men supplied the war effort with food, clothing and money.

The Great Depression

The economic depression that struck the rest of the world in the 1930s hit Prince Edward Island hard. There was a shortage of cash in both rural and urban areas. The value of all farming products was reduced by half or more. Pork, for example, dropped in price from 34 cents a kilogram (15-1/2 cents a pound) to seven (3-1/3) cents. A quantity of potatoes that sold for $1.50 in 1929 was worth six cents in 1932. Fishing people also faced difficult times, with cod and lobsters dropping to half their pre-depression prices.

At the time, 75 percent of the population lived in rural areas, and that fact provided one slightly positive note: since most Islanders lived on farms and grew their own food and gathered their own wood, they had enough to eat and had fuel to keep themselves warm in winter. In the cities, however, people were unemployed, hungry, and often homeless and cold.

Unemployed people on the Island formed the Unemployed Workmen's Association to work together to solve their economic problems. In 1932, this group had a membership of 600. Church organizations and private charities gave clothing, food and coal to those in need, but could not provide enough help for the ever-increasing number of poor and homeless. As the Great Depression went on, people began to demand more help from government.

Some federal and provincial government money was spent on direct relief, but most was spent on work projects. In 1933, for example, government relief work in Charlottetown employed 5853 men who had 16 169 dependents, for a total of 22 000 people who benefitted from government assistance.

Co-operation

Co-operation is important in hard times. An early example is the Farmers' Bank of South Rustico. This bank, founded in 1864 by Father Belcourt, was the smallest chartered bank in British North America and operated much like a modern credit union. After the First World War, the idea of co-operation was spread by people like Dr. John T. Croteau, a professor at St. Dunstan's University and Prince of Wales College. He encouraged Islanders to establish study clubs. Neighbours gathered to discuss what they could do to change or improve their situations. Teachers, priests, ministers, fishermen and farmers talked and socialized. The study groups led to the founding of co-operatives, including the Credit Union League, the Fishermen's Central, the Federation of Agriculture and the Island Co-op Services. By the end of the Second World War, Islanders had

Memorial honouring Islanders who served in the two world wars and the Korean conflict

established egg and poultry co-operatives, potato warehouses, seven fishermen's co-operatives, and 55 local credit unions. The co-operative and credit union movement continues to be a strong feature of Island life.

The Second World War

The Second World War (1939-1945) ended the depression that had gripped the Island and most of the western world. The prices of farm and fish products suddenly increased. New military bases on the Island at St. Eleanors, Mt. Pleasant and Wellington created employment and new prosperity in Prince County.

Nearly 9000 Prince Edward Islanders fought overseas during the Second World War; many of them did not come home. Those who did, and Islanders who had laboured at home to keep farms and services running, would soon find themselves with a whole new set of challenges to face.

CHAPTER 6

Government and Politics

Confederation brought federal representation to Prince Edward Island — six elected members of Parliament (MPs) and four Senators. The number of MPs was reduced to four in 1904, as the population of the other provinces grew much faster than the Island's.

At the provincial level, the government, like that of all the provinces is headed by a Lieutenant-Governor who represents the Queen. The premier, who actually runs the government, is the leader of the party that wins the most seats in the election. The Island's 32-seat Legislative Assembly has one feature that distinguishes it from other provincial legislatures: each of the Island's 16 electoral districts elects two members, one called a councillor, the other an assemblyman or assemblywoman.

Parties, Premiers and Policies

Before it joined Confederation in 1873, Prince Edward Island had been a separate colony for 104 years. Between the years 1851 and 1873, during the first 22 years of responsible government, there had been 12 governments. The province's Liberal and Conservative parties were often filled with quarrelling factions, and politicians frequently switched from one party to the other. Hot arguments took place at the drop of a hat. There was no shortage of opposing views: Protestant versus Catholic, landowner versus tenant, pro-Confederation versus anti-Confederation.

Province House, where the Charlottetown Conference was held and where the provincial legislature still meets

A Robert Harris sketch of an election in Charlottetown in 1872. Elections were lively affairs in the days before voting by secret ballot came to the Island in 1913.

After Confederation, some of the issues changed, but the political style remained much the same. In other provinces, one party and one premier often directed political life for long periods of time. But in Prince Edward Island, the duration of political administrations has generally been rather short. There are two exceptions to this. From 1891 to 1911 and 1935 to 1959 Liberal governments had two long stretches in office. The election of 1935, when the Liberals won every seat in the legislature, was the first-ever "clean sweep" in a Canadian provincial election.

Alex B. Campbell, a Liberal, was premier from 1966 to 1978, a period of enormous economic change on Prince Edward Island. Premier Campbell introduced a 15-year federal-provincial agreement called the Comprehensive Development Plan. This plan was part of a national policy aimed at distributing the benefits of economic growth more evenly among the regions of Canada. Since some regions of the country — the Maritimes, for instance — were relatively poor, and other regions — such as Ontario and Alberta — were relatively rich, the idea was to share the costs of many human

Prince Edward Island boasts one of the country's finest provincial park systems. Seen here: a guided nature walk at Cabot Beach Provincial Park

services programs so that all Canadians would have more equal services and benefits. To achieve this, the federal government would use revenue from the wealthier provinces to support programs that otherwise might have been too expensive for Islanders (and others), programs such as family allowances, unemployment insurance, old age security, the Canada Pension Plan and health care.

In the 1950s, personal income on the Island was just over half the figure for Canada as a whole. Transfer payments, as the cost-sharing was called, soon brought the average personal income of Islanders more in line with that of the rest of Canada. The effect of this policy was a greater loss of independence for many Islanders. This loss was traded off for a better standard of living.

Two Conservative premiers, Walter Shaw and Angus MacLean, represented older Island politics. They sought a return to the traditional farm economy and community life. Their supporters felt the province was a "garden of Eden," a "million-acre farm" on which independent yet community-minded people could shape their own destinies. Angus MacLean, premier from 1979 to 1981, called his politics a "rural renaissance." He and others saw the need for Islanders to regain control of their economic lives. They thought it possible to build another golden era on the Island by respecting the resources of land and sea and developing a sustainable agriculture and aquaculture.

Joseph Ghiz was elected premier in 1986 and again in 1989. In 1993, he was followed by Catherine Callbeck, the first woman in Canada to be elected as a premier. Keith Milligan succeeded her as leader of the Liberal party and premier in October 1996. In the following election, after only 40 days in office, Keith Milligan was defeated by Patrick Binns, leader of the Progressive Conservatives. Dr. Herbert Dickieson became the first New Democratic Party candidate in Island history to win a seat in the provincial legislature.

Local Government

Prince Edward Island has two cities, seven towns, 30 villages and 51 other rural municipalities in its three counties. Municipal government has been established in the province by three acts: the

The Charlottetown City Hall, built in 1883, houses municipal offices, civic courtrooms and the police department.

Charlottetown Act, the Summerside Act, and the Municipalities Act. This last act, passed in 1983, provides direction for 86 incorporated towns and communities. Councils of towns and communities are elected, with a mayor or chairperson as the chief executive officer. Council meetings are open to the public, although committee meetings may be held in private. Municipal powers include garbage collection and disposal, sewage treatment, roads, water, police protection, libraries and public transportation.

Education

During the colonial days, poor families on the Island could not afford to send their children to school. The children of wealthy landowners were instructed by private tutors or were sent to boarding schools off-Island. After 1825, there were schools in each district, but the money provided by the government for teachers' salaries was not enough to encourage a system of education to thrive.

The Free Education Act, passed by the government in 1852, changed the education scene. All children over five years of age, no matter how poor, were able to go to school. Teachers' salaries improved and training was provided at a newly formed Normal School.

The heart of an Island community was often its small, rural school. Concerts, plays, socials, political meetings and many other events took place in the one-room schools. "Each day it was a different student's job to carry a pail of drinking water to the school," Mrs. William "Effie" Campbell wrote about her days in Southwest Lot 16 school in the early 1900s. "There was no plumbing and no electricity. At night when we had concerts, we used lanterns, otherwise we just worked by the natural sunlight streaming in through the windows."

Most one-room schools eventually got indoor plumbing and electricity, but they had no gymnasiums or libraries. Few went beyond grade 8, and teachers' salaries did not reflect the dedicated work they did. The average teacher's salary in 1962 was $2700, less than half the Canadian standard.

Consolidation of the 470 small schools into 57 large ones in 1972 dramatically changed education and community life in the province. Consolidation meant most students had to be bused to school, and so education was removed from each community's centre. However, consolidated schools provided new facilities at a minimal cost, paid for largely by the federal-provincial development agreement. Curriculum planners consulted teachers from all parts of the Island in the development of a revised school curriculum.

In 1995, the school population of 24 622 elementary, junior high and senior high students attended three private and 65 public schools in three school districts, taught by about 1425 teachers.

Higher Education

The Island's first post-secondary institution was Prince of Wales College, founded in 1836. A second institution, St. Dunstan's University, opened in 1855. St. Dunstan's University and Prince of

Left: The old one-room school at Canoe Cove. Although the large, new consolidated schools seem less personal, the Island's student-teacher ratio remains the country's lowest. *Right:* An elementary classroom at the band-operated John J. Sark Memorial school on Lennox Island

Wales joined together in 1969 to become the University of Prince Edward Island. U.P.E.I. offers degrees in arts, science, nursing, education and music.

The Atlantic Veterinary College (A.V.C.), opened in 1986, is the fourth Canadian university to offer a degree in veterinary medicine.

Holland College was named after Samuel Holland, who surveyed the Island in 1764-65. A community college, it was created in 1969 to provide education in applied arts and technology, vocational training and adult education. A School of Justice was established in 1988 as part of the College, with two departments: the Atlantic Police Academy, now based in Summerside, and Justice Training. A language school was established in 1996. Holland College has learning centres located across the Island.

The Right to Vote

Today, every Canadian citizen or British subject who has been resident in the province for six months and who is at least 18 years old is eligible to vote in Prince Edward Island elections. This was not always the case.

Prince Edward Island was the second-last province in Canada to extend the right to vote to women, six years after the first province, and four years after the federal franchise had been granted to all Canadian women.

As elsewhere in Canada, Island women had to fight to change ideas about women's place in society. Elsie Inman and Margaret Rogers Stewart formed the Women's Liberal Club in 1916. Members of this club wrote for advice to Nellie McClung and other suffragists who pioneered the struggle for women's rights on the Canadian prairies. Several years, many petitions and much work later, Premier John Bell extended the franchise to Island women in 1922.

CHAPTER 7

The Island Today

"**W**e're just enough behind to be a little ahead," goes an Island expression. Islanders don't rush to jump on bandwagons and are slow to follow fads and trends. This deliberate slowness to change sometimes infuriates people, but the trait does help Islanders achieve a sense of balance and judgment about which changes to take and which to leave. An example of this habit of "second thinking" is the controversy over a proposal by a high-tech, military-industrial company that wanted to move to the Island.

In 1985, the Prince Edward Island government won a bidding war to have a large, multi-national company, Litton Industries, build a plant in the province. This branch of Litton would make components for a low-level air-defence system. Many Islanders protested the government's decision to bring a war-associated, nuclear-related industry to Prince Edward Island. Litton promised some immediate jobs to Islanders, but it would make no promises about long-term employment.

When concerned citizens protested strongly, the government rethought its decision. "The government wants jobs for Islanders," said Premier Joe Ghiz, "but not at any price. P.E.I. is not a banana republic." Litton Industries went elsewhere.

Until fairly recently, Prince Edward Island was mainly rural in nature. Most people lived in the country and earned their living by farming. There were set ways of doing many tasks, patterns often based on seasons and weather. These patterns have a new-found value in the 1990s, when concern for the earth and "green thinking" have begun to replace unplanned development and progress at any cost.

New London. Despite the fame of its colourful red clay roads, the Island actually has more paved road per capita than any other place in Canada.

The Accelerating Pace of Change

After the Second World War, striking economic, social, political and technological changes in all of Canada affected Prince Edward Island too. Community life and the traditional farm economy began to erode, and the notion that the Island was a garden of Eden began to fade.

During this period, the traditional way of life did not die. Many Islanders still had emotional, historical and practical bonds with the land and sea. It is a telling fact that as late as 1951, the farm horse population on Prince Edward Island was 21 000, and more than 90 percent of all Island farms had horses.

Rural Prince Edward Island was "electrified" beginning in 1953. Electrification meant that farms as well as towns could have washers and dryers, toasters, televisions and all the other modern conveniences. These were powerful sources of change. During this same period, paving the muddy and often undrivable rural roads also brought dramatic changes to farm and small community life. It meant not only that cars and trucks travelled more easily and greater distances to markets, but also that more people could earn their living off the farm, at food processing plants and in the manufacturing and service industries.

Because income on the Island was substantially lower than the national average, however, many Islanders were attracted by better paying and more secure jobs elsewhere. Young people especially went "down the road" to other parts of Canada and to the United States. This affected the emotional as well as the economic climate of the province.

National programs put into place to deal with the problem of regional disparity had far-reaching effects on the Island. The Federal-Provincial Comprehensive Development Plan attempted to bring about a better standard of living by switching people from the primary industries of farming and fishing to industrial, manufacturing and service jobs. In many ways it appeared to work. Between 1951 and 1986, the number of farms fell from 10 137 to 2833. At the same time,

Abandoned farmhouse near Greenwich. Biologist Ian MacQuarrie has described the passing of time on the Island: "The flight from the farm began over a century ago. This receding tide has left the hills dotted with abandoned buildings, old cellars, overgrown gardens and orchards....While the land may still be farmed, house and barn return slowly to the soil from which they were created."

the size of the average farm increased from 44 hectares (108 acres) to 94 hectares (232 acres). Recently, new potato processing plants opened, employing several hundred Islanders.

Land Use

Land has value just for being itself. It also has value as a tourist attraction. The main charm of Prince Edward Island has always been its relatively unspoiled landscapes.

Over the past century, and especially in the last 25 years, tourism has been heavily and successfully promoted on the Island. By now, the tourist industry is the Island's second largest industry, having bumped fishing into third place some years ago.

Tourism brings many economic benefits to the Island, but it also brings the possibility of damage to the natural environment.

Tall, long-rooted marram grass helps keep the north shore sand dunes stable. If the grass is killed by heavy human traffic, the sand can shift and spread, cover over neighbouring farmland and silt up fishing harbours.

Cottages spring up along many stretches of coastline. Fragile dune systems are destroyed by bathers walking to beaches off the beaten paths. Strips of fast-food restaurants and other businesses line roads leading into urban centres. Farmland is bought up for the construction of golf courses and tourist attractions.

A Land Use Commission was set up to deal with problems of land use and misuse. The Commission has stopped some prime agricultural land from being commercially developed. Shorefront cottage development has been halted at times to allow studies into its effects on the land. A law passed in 1972 requires non-residents to apply for cabinet approval for the sale or purchase of property larger than four hectares (ten acres) or having more than 100 metres (330 feet) of shorefront. A decade later, another law limited landholdings by corporations to 1215 hectares (3000 acres). Corporate farms such as McCain Foods and Cavendish Farms are able to lease more than 1215 hectares (3000 acres), and so are still able control large potato-growing farms.

Fixed Links

Before the advent of ferries that could transport railcars, shipping large quantities of goods to and from the mainland was slow and irregular. The first debates about a fixed link with the mainland took place between 1884 and 1914. Some Islanders wanted the Canadian government to build an iron tube through which trains and cars could travel on the bottom of the Northumberland Strait. The difficulties of engineering such a tunnel were too great for it to go into construction, however, and with the building of a new railcar ferry in 1918 demand for a tunnel halted.

Interest in a fixed link — this time in the form of a bridge or a causeway — began again between 1955 and 1965. Work actually started near Borden in the summer of 1965 on the highway approaches to a causeway. But there was opposition from those who thought that the causeway would weaken Prince Edward Island's control over its own affairs. In June 1967, the federal government rejected tenders for the first section of the crossing because projected costs were much higher than expected. Construction was halted, and in 1969 the entire causeway project was shelved.

In the late 1980s and early 1990s, the subject of a link was raised again. Several wealthy private investors competed to bring proposals to the government for a toll bridge or a tunnel. On January 18, 1988, a provincial plebiscite, or special vote, asked: "Are you in favour of a fixed link crossing between Prince Edward Island and New Brunswick?" Only 69 percent of the people voted, a surprisingly low figure in a province that averages an 85-90 percent turnout for general elections. They favoured a fixed crossing by 59 to 41 percent.

Although final approval for any sort of fixed link hinged on the results of environmental studies, construction on the bridge began in 1995. An environmental review committee found that ice buildup around pilings might affect the growing season and might slow down the reproduction rate of lobsters, and damage the spawning grounds of herring. However, the environmentalists were unable to stop construction, and the bridge is scheduled to open in 1997.

The $840 million Confederation Bridge to the mainland has created hundreds of jobs for Islanders and is expected to help increase tourism and other Island industries.

The *Abegweit II*, the largest ship making the ferry run between New Brunswick and the Island, can carry up to 250 cars and 900 passengers.

Renewable Energy on the Island

Prince Edward Islanders pay some of the highest prices in Canada for oil, gas, natural gas and electrical power. This is because there is no oil, hydroelectricity or coal on the Island. New Brunswick supplies some power to the Island via a cable that runs under the Strait of Northumberland.

In recent years, several alternate energy resources have been developed on Prince Edward Island. These include the use of biomass fuels to replace oil, energy-from-waste plants, district heating and wind energy.

Biomass energy comes from plants. It is a form of stored solar energy. Almost half of the province is still covered by forests and woodlots, though many of the trees in these forests are diseased, dead or dying. Dead, diseased and dying trees are excellent material for use as fuel in biomass-burning furnaces. Removal of this kind of tree leaves the stronger trees to develop.

The Department of Agriculture, Fisheries and Forestry has been active in reforestation programs, using high-quality seedlings to plant on land that has been harvested of poor quality trees. Biomass-burning furnaces are in use across the province, heating schools, hospitals, businesses and even individual farms. At the University of Prince Edward Island and in downtown Charlottetown, there are district heating systems that provide heat for many buildings. Pipes carrying hot water run under the streets.

carrying hot water run under the streets. Wood chips, sawdust and municipal waste are the fuel used in the central boiler.

Another district heating system based at the University of Prince Edward Island burns home-grown wood chips and saves 1.1 million litres (290 000 gallons) of oil per year. This project cost $1.87 million (1987 dollars), with $0.64 million from the Canada-Prince Edward Island Alternate Energy Development Agreement and the rest from the P.E.I. Energy Corporation.

More than 30 000 tonnes of waste per year are burned in the Island's energy-from-waste plant, an incinerator, in Parkdale, a suburb of Charlottetown. The plant was opened in 1983, and saves the importing of 2.3 million litres (608 000 gallons) of oil each year. Almost all of the burnable garbage from the Charlottetown area goes to the energy-from-waste plant instead of into landfill. The waste is burned twice at very high temperatures, to control emissions of organic substances. The steam generated by the burning of waste heats the Queen Elizabeth and Hillsborough hospitals.

One very promising renewable energy source for Prince Edward Island is wind power. The wind power map of Canada shows that the Island winds are quite powerful, powerful enough to drive devices that can extract energy from the wind. For a number of years researchers at the Atlantic Wind Test Site at North Cape have conducted experiments with different wind turbines. The people at this research facility hope to develop a storage and delivery system that will suit Prince Edward Island.

In the 1980s and 1990s, much research was conducted by the provincial government on alternate forms of energy such as direct solar power, geothermal energy and small-scale hydroelectric projects.

Multicultural Society

Although about 80 percent of Islanders are of British descent, there is a strong multicultural community on Prince Edward Island. People of more than 60 nationalities live here.

The Micmac were the first inhabitants of the Island. Their story has much in common with the stories of most North American Native peoples. In recent years, there has been a revitalization of the Micmac language and culture on the Island. Micmac people are working to achieve recognition of their inherent right to self-government.

"We've been trying to go the other way in the last 10 to 15 years," says Chief Jack Sark of the Lennox Island Band Council, "to get out from under the dependency poured onto us by the Indian Act. By what act of Parliament or what war did the indigenous people agree to become Canadians?" Chief Sark answers his own question. "Native people had no part in the discussions leading to the British North America Act in 1867. Every aspect of our lives is dictated by legislation imposed by a foreign culture."

Small but important changes of attitude have taken place among non-Native Islanders regarding the Micmac people. A recent incident illustrates the change: when John Joe Sark, a Micmac activist, pointed out that the Charlottetown Rural High School's mascot of a fighting Indian was offensive to many Native people, the school decided to drop the use of the mascot.

The flavour of Island culture is very much affected by all of the nationalities that have settled here. In the early eighteenth century, Acadians settled on Prince Edward Island, followed by Scottish, English and Irish immigrants. American and German people also settled the Island. The early German settlers often changed their names to fit the mostly-British culture: Eichorns became Acorns, Henckells became Jenkins, and Junkers became Younkers.

The Lebanese who settled on the Island sometimes had their Arabic names changed by immigration officers: the surnames Kays and Ghiz are English spellings of the same Arabic name. Lebanese given names also were changed to English versions: Said or Sahlibra became Sam, Labeeb became Larry, Amal became Mel, and Elias became Lewis.

The Island is proud of its heritage of Scottish, Irish and English traditions. In the twentieth century, Dutch, South Asian, Scandinavian, Chinese, Polish, Central American, Somalian, Sri Lankan, Nigerian and many other immigrants also have added their rich cultures to the Island mosaic. Islanders continue to welcome newcomers from all over the world. But today, new arrivals no longer feel they have to change their names and adopt "English" ways. Their cultures flourish in festivals and celebrations across the Island.

Left: **Mrs. Mathilda Lewis in her Lennox Island home, surrounded by symbols of her dual cultural heritage — Micmac and Christian.** *Below:* **Islanders celebrate their cultural roots.**

CHAPTER 8

The Island Economy

Prince Edward Island has no mines or oil wells, no large manufacturing companies, no steel or pulp and paper mills, no oil refineries or automobile plants.

What Prince Edward Island does have is a fairly rich fishing industry, relatively fertile land, growing crafts- and arts-related industries, some high technology industries, and the sorts of landscapes and seascapes that bring hundreds of thousands of tourists to the province summer after summer.

One Potato, Two Potato

In harvest season, stray Sebago, Kennebec, Superior, Russet Burbank, Shepody, Blue, Red Pontiac and Bintje potatoes bounce off the mounded heaps on potato trucks moving from field to warehouse and from warehouse to market. Potatoes strewn along the road may be the only amusing kind of roadkill.

When Prince Edward Island's Stompin' Tom Connors wrote "Bud the Spud," he may have had no idea that the song would become almost an anthem for Islanders. Stompin' Tom did know, however, that potatoes are an essential part of the livelihood and folklore of Prince Edward Islanders.

I'm Bud, the Spud, from the bright red mud
Goin' down the highway smilin'
The spuds are big on back of Bud's rig
They're from Prince Edward Island.

Potato field in bloom, Clyde River

Agriculture remains the most important sector of the Island economy, with potatoes being by far the most important crop and livestock accounting for about 15 percent of farm revenue.

Potatoes are the Island's most important crop, contributing an average of over 50 percent of total farm receipts. In 1995, farmers planted 43 700 hectares (108 000 acres) of potatoes, the largest area ever recorded.

Potatoes are grown for table use, for processing into potato chips and fries, and for seed. Prince Edward Island seed potatoes are exported to the United States, Cuba, Venezuela, Uruguay and a number of European countries whose farmers depend on high-quality, imported seed potatoes to produce their own annual crops.

PVY-n Virus

In the summer of 1989, the seed potato industry on Prince Edward Island was devastated by news that a potato virus (PVY-n) had infected some Island potatoes. First the United States and then the rest of Canada banned the importation of P.E.I. seed potatoes for fear of having their own potatoes infected. Because of the virus, 10 000 hectares (4000 acres) of the total 1991 crop were ploughed down and another 3700 hectares (1500 acres) were not harvested.

In 1992, the National Farmers' Union released a research report that stated, "Farmers have suffered unnecessarily as a result of actions taken by Agriculture Canada regarding decisions relating to PVY-n." The report found there was incorrect or inadequate testing carried out on samples of potatoes suspected of having the virus, and that, in fact, the PVY-n virus had been known to be present in some Ontario potatoes for 30 years. The interesting fact about this particular virus is that it has no harmful effect on the potatoes or on people who eat them, but tobacco growing in fields adjacent to potatoes with PVY-n virus is ruined.

The 1992-93 National PVY-n Eradication Plan involved extensive sampling of potato fields across Canada. Agriculture Canada crews crisscrossed fields in a set pattern to pick leaves. The leaves were then tested to identify fields infested with PVY-n. By 1995, Island farmers were able to sell seed potatoes, and Prince Edward Island regained international markets.

Other Crops and Livestock

Strawberries, raspberries and blueberries grow well on the Island, as do oats, peas, beans, barley and wheat. Most farmers grow all the hay and mixed grain they need for their livestock. Vegetables such as carrots, turnips and cabbages are grown both for local use and export. Although tobacco did well in Island soil, all tobacco farming ceased by 1996 and farmers looked for new cash crops, such as ginseng.

Agriculture Canada has plant and animal research laboratories and farms on the Island. About 80 research scientists and staff generate varieties of cereals and forage legumes suitable for production in the Atlantic provinces. They also work on weed and disease control, land conservation and the development of environmentally sensitive land management practices.

Island farmers raise beef cattle, hogs, poultry and dairy cows. Milk is turned into butter, yogurt, ice cream and cheese at dairies located in Alberton, O'Leary, Summerside, Cavendish, Hunter River, North Wiltshire, Charlottetown, Montague and Souris. Powdered and evaporated milk are exported to Europe and South America. Beef, pork, poultry and eggs are produced mainly for local use.

Over the years Prince Edward Island has had several slogans on its licence plates: "Garden of the Gulf," "Spud Island," and "The Million Acre Farm." These descriptions still portray the Island's present-day landscape, and farming makes up the largest part of the Island's economy. Nevertheless, only a small portion of the population lives on farms. Since the end of the Second World War, the trend has been for traditional, small family farms to give way to larger or incorporated farms and "agribusiness." In 1951, almost half of the Island's population lived on farms; by 1981, this number had dropped to ten percent; and by 1996 only six percent of Islanders lived on farms.

Fishing

Fishing ranks third in importance to the Prince Edward Island economy, accounting for $117 million in total sales. The total weight of groundfish, pelagic fish, shellfish and Irish moss harvested in 1995 was 45.7 million kilograms (101.5 million pounds). Lobster accounted for about 68 percent of this total (valued at $78.4 million).

The Island fishing industry employs about 8265 people in fishing, harvesting and processing. Many others are employed in industries that support the fishing industry, such as vessel construction and outfitting.

The sleek Cape Islander boats of the inshore fishing fleet move out of harbours all along the Island's 1760-kilometre (1000-mile) coastline. Flounder, mackerel, redfish, herring and cod are the main market species, although cod, once unimaginably plentiful, now is scarce. Canadian, Portuguese and other European off-shore fishing vessels use fishing techniques which in effect vacuum the oceans. Baby and juvenile fish weighing less than 200 grams (7 ounces), which should be left to grow and replenish stocks, are taken along with regulation-size fish, sometimes accounting for more than half of a vessel's catch of 300 tonnes.

Over the years, cod have been so overfished that in the summer of 1992 the Canadian minister of fisheries declared a moratorium on cod fishing on the Grand Banks. The decline of the east coast fishery has been felt on Prince Edward Island, though not nearly so dramatically as it has in Newfoundland. Lobster is the mainstay of the Island's fishing industry, and it has been tended more carefully than off-shore species.

Other species important to Island fishing are scallops, oysters, quahaugs, mussels, eels, trout, salmon and Irish moss. Trout, salmon, oysters and mussels are raised by aquaculture, or fish farming. The culture of finfish and shellfish in bays and estuaries

Far left: **This is Malpeque, but the scene — fishing boats in harbour, a row of bait sheds, piles of lobster traps — is characteristic of many of the Island's coastal villages.** *Near left:* **Lobster fishing**

Left: Harvesting Irish moss at Miminegash on the west coast. This useful seaweed is gathered on the beach or raked from the surf after a storm, often with the help of horses. *Right:* Bluefin tuna, caught off the east coast of the Island

and in specially-built ponds and tanks is a growing branch of the fishing industry. The aquaculture industry exports shellfish and finfish to North American and European markets.

Tourist brochures once billed North Lake "the tuna capital of the world" because sport fishing enthusiasts came from around the world to catch bluefin from this tiny port at the eastern end of Prince Edward Island. The average weight of tuna caught off North Lake in 1985 was 471 kilograms (1039 pounds). These enormous bluefin were flown by special refrigerated airplanes to Japan, where they fetched up to $22 a kilogram ($10 a pound) at tuna auctions. Tuna is used for *sushi*, a Japanese delicacy made from raw fish.

In 1974, 1041 tuna were landed and, in 1983, 789. Numbers dwindled each following year until the summer of 1987, when what was thought to be the last bluefin was caught off North Lake. By 1992, the world population of bluefin had declined by 90 percent. And then, in 1995, bluefin appeared once again off the north shore of the Island, and 65 of the giant fish were landed that summer.

Fishing is by nature a seasonal employment. Winter months are a time to repair boats and gear and build new lobster traps, but full-time, paid employment is scarce. Most fishing people collect unemployment insurance benefits in the off-season.

Tourism

It is likely that tourism will soon outrank farming as the Island's main industry. In 1995, the tourist industry contributed about $178 million to the Island's economy. Tourism provides about 18 000 seasonal and permanent jobs, thus employing 18 percent of the provincial work force.

Over the last half-century, Prince Edward Island has become an international tourist destination. The number of visitors grew from 11 000 in 1924 to 278 000 in 1963, then doubled by 1983 and reached 800 000 in 1995. This last figure is nearly six times greater than the number of Island residents. There are about 6000 hotel, motel, cabin and bed-and-breakfast units, 35 private campgrounds, 14 provincial park campgrounds and 3 national park campgrounds in the province. The 18-square-kilometre (seven-square-mile) Prince Edward Island National Park, established on the north shore in 1937, includes 50 kilometres (30 miles) of fine beaches.

Many of the tourists who visit the Island come to see for them-selves the places described so vividly in *Anne of Green Gables* and the home of its author, Lucy Maud Montgomery. The Japanese, in particular, seem to have taken the red-haired orphan to their hearts, and in 1995, more than 25 000 Japanese tourists visited the Island.

Aside from the attraction of being the birthplace of one of the world's favourite authors, Prince Edward Island has historic importance as the "birthplace of Canada." Province House in Charlottetown, where the Fathers of Confederation met to discuss forming a Canadian nation, is a National Historic Site. Tours,

Japanese tourists at Green Gables

interpretive programs, displays and the restored and refurnished legislative council chamber attract visitors from across Canada.

Visitors come not only for Prince Edward Island's literary and historic sites, but also for its leisurely pace of life, the beauty of its natural environment, and the reputation of Islanders as friendly, "down-home" people.

Service Industries

Closely related to the tourist industry are the service industries. Tiny as it is compared to other provinces, Prince Edward Island has its own professional and skilled civil service. As well, several federal government departments such as Veterans' Affairs and the Goods and Services Tax (GST) Branch have moved to the Island. Literally thousands of Islanders are employed providing a wide range of services to the public.

Far left: **Co-op lobster cannery at Judes Point.**
Near left: **Woollen Mill at Bloomfield**

Small Industries and Employment

The craft industry, potato processing plants, dairies and dairyfood processing plants, arts-and-entertainment-related enterprises, and a few high technology businesses are growing in importance to the Island's economy. The Atlantic Canada Opportunity Agency and the Federal-Provincial Cooperation Agreement on Culture brought federal money into the Island economy in the 1980s and 1990s.

Nonetheless, during the 1980s and early 1990s, unemployment gradually rose to about 20 percent, a rate similar to that of Newfoundland, New Brunswick and Nova Scotia, but nearly double the national average.

A promising note about the Island's employment scene is the success of many small, locally run businesses, especially since 1987. These companies include retail, craft, computer and software stores, publishing houses, clothing and custom sewing shops and repair services.

CHAPTER 9

Arts, Crafts and Recreation

Prince Edward Island does not have spectacular scenery like British Columbia. In general, its residents are not flamboyant and their customs are not especially colourful. Rather, there is a quiet beauty about the place and an intriguing comfort to be had from the Island's smallness. One can get to know the entire province — its hills, valleys and beaches, its weather and wildlife, its communities and folklore. Prince Edward Island can provide a measure of familiarity and calm in a sometimes very unsettling world. Many artists and craftspeople thrive in this kind of setting.

Crafts

There is a strong tradition of craftwork in the province. Using dyed porcupine quills, the Micmac wove beautiful designs to decorate clothing, baskets and other items. With the introduction of European trade beads, they added beadwork to their fine and complicated designs. Micmac still weave baskets in the traditional way, using *withe*, or strips of ash.

The early European settlers brought with them woodworking, quilting, stitching and weaving skills from the old country. In the eighteenth century, every farm family made everything that was required to satisfy basic needs for shelter, food and clothing. Women and men sheared sheep each spring, and cleaned, carded, spun, dyed, and wove the wool into blankets, coverlets and lengths for clothing. Farmers sowed flaxseed, tended and harvested the crop, and processed flax in a similar fashion to wool.

A production of *Anne of Green Gables* at the Confederation Centre of the Arts

In recent years crafts have been making an important contribution to the Island's economy. Seen here, *clockwise from left:* Quilters at work; Micmac birchbark and porcupine quill boxes; dried apple granny doll

Mass production of goods changed the traditional practices, and the craft tradition on Prince Edward Island — as elsewhere in the western world — declined during the early twentieth century. During the last 20 years, however, there has been a rekindling of interest in heritage and traditional crafts. At present, there are 18 craft guilds on the Island. Pottery, woodwork, glasswork, weaving, quilting, stitchery, metalwork and leatherwork are produced in Island homes, small shops and studios. The P.E.I. Crafts Council has about 120 members. It sponsors a year-round craft shop and an annual four-day Christmas craft fair in Charlottetown. Many craftspeople working with materials such as metal, wood and fabric use designs and skills of early inhabitants of the Island. The items they make are popular with tourists, and cottage craft industries have become important to the province's economy.

Music

Since about 60 percent of the population of Prince Edward Island is of Celtic origin, there is a strong legacy of Scottish and Irish music here. A musical gathering is called by its Gaelic name, a *ceilidh* (pronounced KAY-ly). The old songs are still sung on the Island, often with local variations. It is rare to attend a house party where there is not at least one fiddler in the kitchen. Bagpiping and fiddling thrive, and in Summerside, the College of Piping and Celtic Performing Arts of Canada offers courses in piping, drumming, highland dancing, stepdancing and fiddling.

The University of Prince Edward Island has a small but active music department, and there are adult and children's choirs throughout the province. The Prince Edward Island Symphony has an annual subscription series which often fills the largest theatre on the Island. In 1978 public school teachers Jenet Evers and John Clement began a music program to encourage students to play stringed instruments. Hundreds have taken the program over the years, and at any given time about 240 string players are engaged with a group called Singing Strings. An off-shoot of the school program is the Singing Strings Ensemble, whose members have performed across Canada. Music festivals and competitions in public and high schools are held annually in conjunction with national music festivals.

There are several small recording studios in Prince Edward Island whose managers have encouraged traditional, country and folk musicians by producing, recording and promoting their work.

A large component of the Island's many summer festivals is music — Scottish, Irish, Acadian, folk, bluegrass, traditional, rock and roll, and country music. A simple listing of some of the events from the tourist guide gives a good idea of Islanders' love of music:

Rollo Bay Fiddle Festival, Sound of Music Festival, A Scottish Ceilidh, Triple Threats Musical Theatre Summer School, Bluegrass Festival, Heart of Rock and Roll, 15th Annual Outdoor Scottish Fiddle and Dance Festival, Jamboree Atlantique de Violoneux (Atlantic Fiddlers' Jamboree), 20th Anniversary Celebrations of P.E.I. Scottish Fiddlers and Ceilidh Dancers Association.

Dance

The Celtic heritage is obvious in the Prince Edward Island dance scene as well. Individual teachers and private schools offer courses in highland dancing, Scottish country and Irish dancing, and stepdancing. Acadian stepdancing is also taught and practised in the province, and there are a number of modern dance and ballet schools such as Dance Umbrella and Charlottetown Ballet Theatre.

Below: **Rollo Bay Fiddle Festival.**
Right: **Acadian dancers.**
Bottom right: **Young pipers**

Touring companies such as the Winnipeg Royal Ballet, the National Ballet and Les Grands Ballets usually perform in Charlottetown when they tour the Atlantic region.

Theatre and Film

Plays and concerts have long been an integral part of community life on the Island. Until 1971, each community had its own one- or two-room school where residents held concerts or performed plays. The Victoria Playhouse in Victoria-by-the-Sea, the King's Playhouse in Georgetown, originally built in 1898 and rebuilt in 1984 after a fire, and the Wanda Wyatt Performing Arts Centre in Summerside continue a vital Island theatre tradition. An annual community theatre festival draws entries from across the province, while Theatre Prince Edward Island provides education, performance and technical expertise to the Island's theatre community. At Mont-Carmel in the main Acadian region of the province and at the Carre-four de l'Isle Saint Jean in Charlottetown, the lively tradition of French-language theatre continues.

Left: **The King's Playhouse in Georgetown is a faithful reproduction of the 19th-century Town Hall, designed by William Harris, which burned down in 1982.** *Below:* **A scene from** *The Victoria Playhouse Kids' Show*

The Charlottetown Festival provides Islanders and visitors with a variety of musical theatre. It opened in 1965 with a musical play based on L. M. Montgomery's *Anne of Green Gables*, and by now a summer without Norman and Elaine Campbell and Don Harron's version of *Anne* would be unthinkable for many Islanders and tourists.

There is a growing population of film and video artists on the Island. Brian Pollard, Kent Martin, John Hopkins, JoDee Samuelson, Lee Fleming and other local filmmakers have produced works that have received national recognition. The Island Media Arts Co-op trains new filmmakers and helps established film and video artists to produce their own work.

Architecture

Aside from a handful of native red sandstone buildings, most houses, churches and barns on Prince Edward Island are wooden. Architectural styles of homes still standing from the very early 1800s reflect the Acadian, English, Irish, Scottish or American influences of the builders. Between 1830 and 1860, most houses were a storey-and-a-half, with small central dormers. In the 1860s, Islanders tended to build simple rectangular houses with centre gables and steep roofs, or Italian-style square ones with flat roofs. By the end of the nineteenth century, the L-shaped house was common and remains the most familiar farmhouse type.

Undoubtedly the most impressive building on the Island is Province House in Charlottetown. It is a neo-classical, three-storey building made with Wallace stone from Nova Scotia, designed by local architect Isaac Smith. Another architect who had an enduring influence on Prince Edward Island and Maritime architecture was William Critchlow Harris, brother of painter Robert Harris. William Critchlow Harris designed outstanding markets, theatres and churches, many of which remain today.

Visual Arts

Island painter Robert Harris was president of the Royal Canadian Academy of Art for 13 years and, according to some, was the most influential artist in the country. Harris is probably best known for his commissioned work, completed in 1884, *The Fathers of Confederation*. To paint this group portrait of the men who had met in Charlottetown twenty years earlier, Harris collected photographs of dead "Fathers" and descriptions of them from colleagues, and he met with those still living to sketch them and make notes of their colouring, hand size and other details that helped him portray them as they had been in 1864.

Top left: The Local Stars **by Robert Harris, the Island's most famous painter.** *Bottom left: Sunset P.E.I.* **by Erica Rutherford.** *Below:* **Brian Burke's** *The Poet,* **a portrait of Milton Acorn**

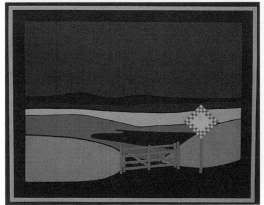

Many artists of national and international reputation live and work on Prince Edward Island. Hilda Woolnough, Brian Burke, Erica Rutherford, Daphne Irving, Ben Kinder, Brenda Whiteway, Ambika Gail Rutherford and Henry Purdy are a few who have helped create a spirited arts scene on the Island.

The Eptek National Exhibition Centre, Princetown Gallery, Confederation Centre Art Gallery and Museum, Ellen Creek Gallery, Pavilloner Art Gallery, Ros Math'ian Art Gallery, and private studios and shops provide Island and touring artists with places to exhibit their work.

Literature

Island writer Lucy Maud Montgomery has had as indelible an effect on Prince Edward Island as the Island itself had on her writing. Her fictional Avonlea, based on real-life Cavendish, first came alive in *Anne of Green Gables*. When the story of the endearing orphan, Anne Shirley, was published in 1908, Montgomery earned a place in the hearts of readers young and old around the world. The novel and its sequels have been translated into more than 40 languages and published in many editions all over the world. Movies, plays and television series have been based on *Anne of Green Gables* and other Montgomery works, such as *The Story Girl.* Uncountable crafts, motels, fastfood places, corner stores and children have been named after Montgomery's characters.

A second major literary figure on Prince Edward Island was Milton Acorn, one of Canada's outstanding poets, whose love for his Island home was a touchstone in his poetry as well as in his life. Believing that he had been shamefully overlooked for the Governor General's Award for poetry in 1970, a group of poets including Irving Layton, Eli Mandel and Margaret Atwood awarded Acorn a thousand dollars and a medal inscribed "The People's Poet." In 1975, Acorn received the Governor General's Award for his collection, *The Island Means Minago*.

Many other writers, either Island-born or "from away," contribute to a vibrant literary scene. These include journalists and nonfiction writers, poets such as John Smith, Joseph Sherman, Richard Lemm, Lesley-Anne Bourne and Frank Ledwell, fiction writers, such as J.J. Steinfield, Michael Hennessey, playwrights Kent Stetson, Eliza Jane Wilson and David Moses, and many others.

In the 1970s, writer Reshard Gool and artist Hilda Woolnough were at the heart of a literary revival on Prince Edward Island. They founded Square Deal Press, which published a newspaper, *The Broad-Axe*, whose motto was, "Hew to the line and let the chips fall where they may." Square Deal also published volumes of poetry, short stories and folklore. The Woolnough-Gool house in Charlottetown became a meeting place for writers and artists, and in summer their music and poetry series brought artists to the Island from across Canada. Gool and Woolnough built a gallery and studios next to their house. For many years, local artists displayed their work, and poets and musicians performed in the Gallery on Demand, known as GOD.

Several publishing houses and organizations, such as Ragweed Press and the Institute of Island Studies, have active publishing programs. *The Island Magazine* published by the P.E.I. Museum and Heritage Foundation, marks its twentieth anniversary in 1997. *ARTSAtlantic* began publishing its subscription quarterly in 1977. *Common Ground*, published by the Women's Network, celebrates 15 years in print in 1997. Other periodicals published on the Island include *Abegweit Review, Island Naturalist, Eco-News* and *Kindred Spirits*.

The Prince Edward Island Council of the Arts has played a significant role in the support and development of all the arts over the past 30 years.

Sports

Prince Edward Islanders like sports. Nearly every community has organized sports events such as skating, hockey, baseball and

Above: There are eight 18-hole and four 9-hole golf courses on the Island, the first of which was established in 1906. *Right:* Tomorrow's champs. *Inset:* Harness racing has long been one of the Island's favourite sports.

soccer. Individuals are involved with track and field and swimming events and squash and racquetball tournaments. Prince Edward Island hosted the 1991 Canada Winter Games, for which a number of new sport facilities were built. Islanders such as John Chabot, Gerard Gallant, Forbes Kennedy, Allan MacAdam, Bobby and Billy

MacMillan, Don Simmons, Errol Thompson and Rick Vaive have played in the NHL.

Harness racing is an extremely popular sport on the Island. Many people consider Joe O'Brien to have been the greatest trainer and driver of harness horses in the world. He set the world's pacing record at 1:52, driving a horse named Steady Star.

Prince Edward Island Champions

George Godfrey was an African-Islander born in 1852 in the part of Charlottetown called "the Bog." He moved to Boston and had a distinguished boxing career. The famous John L. Sullivan, the white heavyweight champion, refused to fight him. In 1883, Godfrey, who fought under the nickname "Old Chocolate," was American Black heavyweight champion.

Michael Thomas was a Micmac from Lennox Island and an outstanding long-distance runner. He won nearly every major distance race in eastern Canada between 1910 and 1912.

In 1951, Evelyn Henry was the first person to swim the Northumberland Strait. Barb McNeill, another fine Island swimmer, conquered the Strait in 1987. In August 1988, McNeill tried twice to swim the English Channel. The second attempt ended when she voluntarily climbed onto a boat to give CPR to another swimmer who was in trouble. McNeill successfully swam the English Channel the following year, and she is one of several women inducted into the Prince Edward Island Sports Hall of Fame.

Charles Ernest Ryan was known as the Island's "Mr. Baseball." A leading member of the Island's Black community, he became an all-star catcher and pitcher and then went on to coach dozens of teams. After his death, the Charlottetown Baseball League changed its name to the Charlie Ryan Memorial Baseball League.

In the 1992 Albertville Olympics, David MacEachern of Charlottetown and his team won a bronze medal in luge racing, the first Olympic medal ever won by an Islander.

CHAPTER 10
A Tour of the Island

Prince Edward Island is the only province or territory in Canada small enough to tour in one day.

Nonetheless, there are still some residents who rarely travel much beyond their own community and its closest urban centre — Summerside or Charlottetown. Islanders themselves often make fun of their sense of smallness and small-town way of thinking. There's a story told about a man from "up west" who lived on a farm near Alberton. One day he had a visitor from "down east." "I hear tell," the man remarked to the visitor, "they got a store in Charlottetown that sells nothing but shoes."

The lines that divide Prince Edward Island into three counties slice across the province from north to south. In the language of Islanders, most of Prince County is known as "up west," and any place east of Charlottetown, including all of Kings County, is known as "down east." It is fairly easy to guess that the people who first used these terms must have lived in Queens County — the centre from which up and down were measured. While any place west of Summerside is generally called "up west," Tignish was once "away up west."

As good a place as any to start a tour of the Island is in its only city, Charlottetown. Then, a visitor might head east and follow the three scenic routes — the Kings Byway, Blue Heron and Lady Slipper Drives — that circle the Island's three counties.

Charlottetown

Most cities and towns in North America experienced huge changes

Overleaf: **New London Bay.** *Insets, top to bottom:* **Naufrage Harbour (***naufrage* **is French for shipwreck); fiddlers at sunset; West Point Lighthouse**

Top: Aerial view of Charlottetown. St. Dunstan's Basilica, seen in the centre, is one of Canada's largest churches.
Left: Government House. *Above:* One of the many attractive residential streets in the heart of the city

in shopping habits during the era of large mall development in the 1970s and 1980s. For quite a few years there was a drain on downtown Charlottetown, to the extent that even the movie houses moved to the malls. However, a strong downtown business group worked to bring more life to the city core in the early 1990s. Art galleries, cafés, lounges, craft shops and sensitive restoration of historical buildings make Charlottetown a lively and attractive place.

The population of the actual city is about 30 000. If all of the surrounding communities are included, however, the figure is close to 55 000, or about 40 percent of the population of the Island.

Because of the Charlottetown Conference in September 1864 and its role in Confederation, Charlottetown is known as the "birthplace of Canada," and the province is sometimes called "the cradle of Confederation." The building in which the delegates to the Charlottetown Conference met, Province House, looks much as it did over a century ago. Completed in 1847, Province House is a national historic site.

The Confederation Centre of the Arts opened in 1964 on the site of the historic farmers' market. It is here that each summer the Charlottetown Festival performs *Anne of Green Gables*, a musical play based on L.M. Montgomery's novel. The Confederation Centre Art Gallery and Museum is part of the sprawling, concrete arts centre. It is the largest art museum east of Montreal, with collections of paintings, drawings, sculptures, and manuscripts, including many original, hand-written manuscripts by Lucy Maud Montgomery. The Robert Harris Gallery at the Centre has a large collection of Harris' fine portraits, sketches and notebooks.

A walking tour of the provincial capital reveals street after tree-lined street of wooden houses, most of Victorian architecture. The Hillsborough River and Bay wrap around the city, so water views are common. At the edge of Victoria Park in the southwest part of the city is Fanningbank, or Government House, designed by architect Isaac Smith as the official residence of the Lieutenant-Governor. Evenings, hundreds of crows gather in the tall birch and spruce trees in the woods behind this elegant home. Victoria Park has been a favourite roosting site of crows for more than a hundred years.

Kings Byway Drive

The Hillsborough Bridge is the only direct way to get from Charlottetown to the southeastern part of the Island. Before the first

Above: The Micmac name for Murray Harbour was *Eskwâdec*, "the fishing place." The village is still home to a busy fishing fleet of some 35 boats.
Left: Built in 1846, the lighthouse on Point Prim is the oldest on the Island.
Inset: Orwell Corner Historic Village

bridge was built across the Hillsborough River in 1905, a paddle-wheel ferry powered by horses crossed four times daily between the city and Southport.

The Northumberland Strait lies on the south side of the Island, with many bays that cut into the land and make the coastline ragged. Lighthouses at the tips of headlands mark the way for fishing and cargo vessels. There are many stories of the sightings of ghost ships in the wide, shallow bays of the Strait. Through the years many people have reported seeing a flaming ship in Pownal Bay, believed to be a vessel that burned during a terrible storm 150 years ago.

Orwell Corner Historic Village is a preserved nineteenth-century Island village. Pioneers from Scotland and Ireland settled at this crossroads and farmed the surrounding area. A farmhouse with post office, general store and dressmaker's shop is furnished as it would have been in 1864. There is a church, school, blacksmith's shop, shingle mill and a community hall where *ceilidhs* are held on Wednesday nights.

Close by Orwell Corner is the homestead of Sir Andrew Macphail, a medical doctor and writer who was an early supporter of sustainable farming and good forest practices. His 56-hectare (140-acre) homestead has been restored and houses a library and historical objects. Outside, there are streamside nature trails, an ecological forestry project and a wildflower garden.

The South Shore

One of the finest views of the Northumberland Strait is from the Point Prim Lighthouse, built in 1845 by Isaac Smith, the architect who designed Province House and Fanningbank in Charlottetown.

The water of the Northumberland Strait along the south shore of the Island is warmer than along the north shore. Lobsters moult or shed their exoskeletons twice a summer in the Strait, which means they grow faster than they do in the colder Gulf of St. Lawrence waters.

Three Rivers

The area where the Cardigan, Brudenell and Montague rivers flow into Cardigan Bay was settled early in the eighteenth century. It was here that French-born Jean Pierre Roma founded a colony called Trois Rivières (Three Rivers) in 1732. Roma and his 300 settlers built a pier near present-day Brudenell. They cleared the woods, removed 6000 or so stumps, levelled the land, built houses, planted gardens and fished the rich sea.

Roma's dream of building a prosperous settlement turned into a nightmare. Fires destroyed most of the crops in 1736. Two years later a plague of field mice ate the entire crop. Then, a vessel carrying cargo to the new colony was shipwrecked. Finally, in 1745, the British attacked and destroyed the settlement.

In the nineteenth century, logging and shipping were the main bases of the economy in the area. Today farming, tourism and fishing are the backbones of the economy. The towns of Montague, Cardigan and Georgetown are the commercial centres of this part of Kings County.

Souris

The Magdalen Islands and Newfoundland ferries dock in Souris, a town named for early plagues of mice (*souris* is French for mouse) which hit the eastern part of the Island especially hard. In 1724, 1728, 1738 and 1749, a species of forest-dwelling mouse with black fur, short legs and flat paws swarmed out of the woods and ate all of the Acadians' precious crops and stored grain. There are accounts of rivers being so choked with bodies of dead mice that ships were slowed. In trying to cross the river, swarms of mice would push those in front of them into the water, with wave after wave of rodents adding to the pile.

East of Souris, on a site overlooking the Northumberland Strait, is the Basin Head Fisheries Museum, an interpretive centre about the Island's inshore fishing industry. Outside the museum is an old cannery, a saltbox factory and reconstructed bait sheds. The dunes along this stretch of shore are wide and relatively isolated, and the beach sand is squeaky underfoot, hence its name "singing sands."

Souris today is a busy fishing port and the terminal for the ferry that links Prince Edward Island with the Magdalen Islands.

East Point

The East Point Lighthouse was built in 1867. From its 21-metre-high (64-foot) octagonal tower it is possible to see "the meeting of the tides," where the waters of the Gulf of St. Lawrence meet those of the Northumberland Strait.

From East Point to Cable Head along the north shore is a wild and beautiful stretch of land. Many red clay lanes lead from the main road directly to the sea. In season, wild strawberries, blueberries and raspberries grow along these quiet, old shore roads.

West of Cable Head is an area called Greenwich where the dune system is extraordinary, with some of the highest dunes on the Island. There are archaeological sites of proto-Micmac settlement on this point of land. The Greenwich headland protects St. Peter's Bay and the village of St. Peter's from the often harsh north winds.

Hillsborough

The Hillsborough River, one of Canada's 'heritage rivers,' flows from its source near Head of Hillsborough to Mount Stewart, where the river widens and continues to widen all the way to Charlottetown. This waterway was one of the main routes of travel used by the Micmac and early settlers. It is still a fine river for canoeing, though there are some fierce currents caused by tides where the river opens into Hillsborough Bay.

Blue Heron Drive

At Tracadie Cross, the Kings Byway angles away from the Hillsborough River and cuts cross country to Grand Tracadie and Dalvay, where Prince Edward Island National Park begins. This 40-kilometre (24-mile) stretch of coastline attracts half a million tourists a year to the Island. The Blue Heron Drive joins the Kings Byway near Brackley Beach.

Many species of shorebirds pass through or live along the inland bays, woodland and pond environments in this region. Great blue herons, piping plover, and numerous waterfowl, woodland and song birds nest here.

Above: **A stretch of red beach and cliffs in Prince Edward Island National Park.** *Left:* **The stone cellar of the Cavendish farmhouse where Lucy Maud Montgomery lived for many years and where she wrote** *Anne of Green Gables*

There is a cluster of communities on the north shore where Acadians settled and where the influence of Acadian culture and language is still strong. Rustico Island, Rustico Bay, North Rustico, North Rustico Harbour, South Rustico, Anglo Rustico, and Rusticoville all got their name from René Rassicot, who came from Normandy in 1724. The Micmac name for the Rustico Bay area was *Tabooetooetun,* "having two outlets." One of the outlets to Rustico Bay was plugged up when a causeway was built from Brackley Beach to Rustico Island in the 1960s. The closing off of this natural flow of water in and out of the bay has caused enormous erosion of the end of Rustico Island and the silting in of the North Rustico Harbour. The almost daily changes to the shoreline around Rustico Bay provide an opportunity to study the environmental effects of humanmade obstructions in the natural world.

Cavendish is the centre of the universe for many L.M. Montgomery fans who travel from around the world to see the homeplace of the famous author. The site of Montgomery's

Cavendish homestead is a quiet spot, with the old apple trees still blooming around the sandstone cellar that is all that remains of the house where Montgomery wrote *Anne of Green Gables*. A great-grandson of Montgomery's grandparents still lives with his family on the homestead.

Park Corner

The Campbell house at Park Corner was a special place for Lucy Maud Montgomery. Here she spent her summers as a young girl. "This is certainly the greatest house in the world for fun," she wrote in her journal. "We have had so many jolly rackets here that the very walls seem to be permeated with the essence of 'good times.'"

Mrs. Ruth Campbell, a relative of Montgomery's family, lives in the old Campbell house at Park Corner. Part of the house is a museum, furnished as it was when Montgomery had her "jolly rackets" there. Each year on July 5, the author's marriage to Reverend Ewan Macdonald is re-enacted in the house at Park Corner, the site of the original wedding.

Below: **French River is just one of many charming villages that lie along the Blue Heron Drive.** *Right:* **The recently restored St. Mary's Roman Catholic Church at Indian River was designed by Island architect William Harris.**

Left: Summerside is the main commercial and service centre for the western end of the Island.
Right: St. Mary's Anglican Church, Summerside. Today's brick structure replaces a wooden one that was destroyed by fire in 1905.

Summerside

Summerside is the Island's second largest urban centre. It has a population of about 8000, double that if surrounding communities are included. In 1989 the Canadian Forces Base at Summerside was closed. The base had been a strong part of Summerside area's economy since the Second World War. Many people lost jobs, the price of houses dropped and a general depression swept over the town. But residents got together to plan their future and to put pressure on the federal government to help western Prince Edward Island. Within a few years, an aircraft manufacturing plant was established in the former air base, and the federal government decided to move a major tax office there.

The shipbuilding industries and silver fox farming that made Summerside prosper in the nineteenth and early twentieth centuries are gone, but mansions built with ship and fox money still give the town a look of wealth and prosperity. The excellent harbour at Summerside is a major shipping port for Island potatoes.

The South Shore Again

East of Summerside is the Bedeque Peninsula. Here dairy, hog and potato farms run right to the water's edge. At low tide it is possible to walk from Lower Bedeque across sandbars to Holman's Island in Summerside Harbour. *Eptek,* the Micmac word for "the hot place," was changed by French settlers to *Bedeque.* Along with Summerside, Bedeque has perhaps the warmest water on the Island.

Until the new Confederation Bridge opens in 1997, the main transportation links between Prince Edward Island and the mainland are ferries that dock at the port town of Borden-Carleton. Marine Atlantic operates a year-round service from Borden-Carleton to Cape Tormentine, New Brunswick, for passengers, cars and trucks. In winter ice-breaking ferries crack the thick ice of the Strait to maintain the mainland's link with the Island.

Cape Traverse was used during the last century as the terminal for crossings to the mainland. At one time there was a post office and hotel at Cape Traverse Landing, which is closer to New Brunswick than the present-day terminal at Borden-Carleton.

Blue Heron Drive winds through Victoria-by-the-Sea, the Argyle Shore and Canoe Cove to Fort Amherst and Port LaJoye, the original capital of the Island. From here, it is just a short distance across the harbour to Charlottetown, though by car the trip takes half an hour.

The interior of Queens County has rolling hills covered with farms and thick woodlands. Some of the old clay roads that wind through this part of the province look untouched by the twentieth century. These roads, recently protected by law and honoured as heritage roads, are sunken below the level of adjacent fields and are often canopied by the branches of tall trees.

West River at sunrise

Lady Slipper Drive

The Lady Slipper Drive west of Summerside branches to the north at Miscouche and follows the curves of Malpeque Bay. Malpeque oysters, farmed and harvested in the bay, have a reputation of being the best in the world.

At Green Park Provincial Park near Tyne Valley, there is a shipbuilding museum. Outside the interpretive centre is a restored shipyard from the era of wooden ships, with a saw pit, blacksmith shop and the ribs of an old sailing ship.

Lennox Island

Two hundred and fifty members of the Lennox Island Band of Micmac live on the reserve at Lennox Island. Few speak the Micmac language, but elders have kept the language and stories alive, and the last decade has seen something of a recovery of the language and culture.

The Lennox Island Band has a commercial peat moss operation, an oyster co-op and a handcraft outlet. In a small museum there are murals of Micmac legends.

Green Park. From the widow's walk of his large Victorian House, James Yeo was able to watch over his shipyard, which has been recreated as a shipbuilding museum.

Alberton, Tignish, and the Western Shore

The largest communities in West Prince County are Alberton and Tignish, both of which have populations of about 1000. The people in both these towns and the surrounding communities depend mainly on fishing for their livelihoods. Lobster and inshore fish are not the only profitable harvests of the sea, however. Irish moss, a valuable seaweed, is gathered from the shores after storms when it has been washed in from seabeds. Horses are used to rake the moss from the surf. A substance found in Irish moss, carrageenan, is used as a thickener in ice cream, medicines and toothpaste.

Kildare Capes and other sandstone cliffs along the coastline between Alberton and North Cape are worth investigating. Strong wind and wave action wears away the mud and soft stone of the coastline, leaving unusual capes and stark grass-topped bluffs.

Far right: **Kildare Capes.** *Right:* **Acadians of the Evangeline Region celebrate the harvest and their heritage at Abram-Village.** *Below:* **Aerial view of Mont-Carmel**

The Evangeline Region

The Acadian Pioneer Village in Mont-Carmel gives a good idea of life in this region in the early 1800s. The main source of income here is inshore fishing. The fishing grounds where most of the residents of the Evangeline district work are in Egmont and Bedeque bays.

The entire Evangeline area has its own flavour. Houses are painted in bright colours, restaurants serve traditional Acadian food, and theatres feature Acadian drama and music. A new museum in Miscouche has paintings, quilts, manuscripts and artifacts that document Acadian history.

A quick tour of Prince Edward Island can provide only a glimpse of what Lucy Maud Montgomery called its "peculiar, indefinable charm." Even that glimpse, however, helps one understand the strength of feeling it inspires in those who know it well. It is a small place, with small changes of landscape and relatively small farms. By some quirk of nature, there are almost no valuable mineral deposits here, and because its land mass and population are tiny, heavy industries have not been very interested in moving to the Island. Even with huge changes over the past half century, Prince Edward Islanders are still very bound to the sea and to the land, and they have a deep appreciation for their small Island home.

Facts
at a Glance

General Information

Entered Confederation: July 1, 1873

Origin of Name: Named in 1799 for Prince Edward, the Duke of Kent, son of King George III

Provincial Capital: Charlottetown, incorporated in 1855.

Provincial Nicknames: "Spud Island," "The Million Acre Farm," "The Garden Province," "*Abegweit*," "*Minegoo*." Most residents simply call their home "The Island."

Provincial Flag: The official seal adopted in 1769 was a large oak tree representing the mother country with a smaller oak in its shadow representing the Island of St. John. When the provincial coat of arms was adopted in 1905, the smaller oak became three small oaks to represent the Island's three counties. The provincial flag, adopted in 1964, is of similar design, with a lion in gold on a background of red and the large oak and three saplings in green and brown growing from a green island on a background of white.

Motto: *Parva sub Ingenti*—Latin for "The small under the protection of the great."

Provincial tartan: The Prince Edward Island tartan was designed in 1960 by Mrs. Jean Reed of Covehead and adopted after a province-wide contest. The tartan colours are reddish-brown to represent the redness of the soil; green to represent grass and trees; white for the caps on the waves; and yellow for the sun.

Provincial flower: Lady's slipper

Provincial bird: Blue jay

Provincial tree: Northern red oak

Provincial song: "The Island Hymn" by L.M. Montgomery

Population

Population: 137 316 (July 1996)

Population distribution:
(1991 census)

Urban: 39.9%

Rural: 60.1%

Kings County	19 328
Queens County	67 196
Prince County	43 241

Population density: 22.9 per km2 (59 per sq.mi)

Population growth:

1848	62 678
1871	94 021
1891	109 078
1901	103 259
1911	93 728

1921	88 600
1931	88 000
1941	95 000
1951	98 400
1961	105 000
1971	112 000
1981	123 000
1991	129 765
1996	137 316

Cities and Towns:

Charlottetown	31 385
Summerside	13 620
Stratford	5395
Cornwall	4050
Montague	1901
Souris	1333
Kensington	1332
Alberton	1068
Georgetown	716
Borden-Carleton	436

Geography

Borders: Prince Edward Island lies in the Gulf of St. Lawrence and is separated from New Brunswick and Nova Scotia by the Strait of Northumberland.

Area: 5660 km^2 (2185 sq.mi.)

Length: 224 km (140 mi.)

Width: 6-64 km (4-40 mi.)

Highest point: 139.5 m (458 ft.) at Springton, Queens County

Lowest point: Sea level

Rank in area among provinces: Tenth

Rivers and lakes: The longest rivers are the Hillsborough, North and East rivers which all empty into Charlottetown Harbour. Most of the Island's rivers are salt creeks because tides flow into their mouths. There are a few small fresh water ponds and lakes and many saltwater lagoons enclosed by sand dunes.

Coasts: The entire coastline (1770 km/1100 mi.) is indented with bays and tidal inlets. On the north shore sand dunes block many of these inlets, preventing large vessels from entering. On the south shore there are a number of good harbours.

Islands: There are many small islands off the P.E.I. coast, including St. Peter's Island, Lennox Island and Governor's Island.

Topography: Most of the Island consists of rolling land, with two distinctly hilly regions — one in southern Kings County, the other in western Queens. About 60% of the province is suitable for cultivation. Along the coast, there are many stretches of fine, sandy beaches as well as stretches of sandstone cliffs eroded by wind and wave action.

The division of the Island into lots, or townships, in 1767 still affects the overall look of the land: there are neat rectangles of fields, woodlots and forests all across the Island, with many roads following the borders of lots. The regular pattern is interrupted by long tidal inlets, deep bays and streams.

Climate: Masses of air from the mainland move east across the Island, but the sea moderates their impact.

The relatively warm water of the Gulf of St. Lawrence keeps winter from arriving as early as it does in other Maritime provinces. On the other hand, the ice that forms in the Gulf slows the arrival of spring.

Winters can be stormy, with frequent violent gales. Annual snowfall is about 300 cm (120 in.). The coldest month is January and the warmest is July. The average frost-free period is 140-160 days. The annual rainfall is about 800 mm (30 in.). Summers are sunny and pleasant, with an average temperature of 22°C (72°F).

Nature

Trees: Alder, ash, aspen, birch, cedar, chestnut, elm, fir, hemlock, maple, oak, pine, spruce and willow

Wild plants: Irish moss, marram grass, mayflower, trillium, purple-fringed orchid, purple violet, wild strawberry, lady's slipper

Animals: Beaver, muskrat, raccoon, red fox, red squirrel, mink, weasel, coyote, snowshoe hare, striped skunk

Birds: More than 300 species have been recorded on the Island, including many water and shore birds, hawks and harriers, owls and songbirds. Great blue herons are a common sight, and the piping plover nests on the north shore.

Fish: Brook trout, rainbow trout, Atlantic salmon, cod, mackerel, red fish, hake, flounder, herring, smelts, gaspereaux, eels

Shellfish: Lobster, scallops, oysters, mussels, bar clams, quahaugs, snow crab, rock crab, softshell crab

Sea mammals: Harbour seal, grey seal, harp seal, white-sided dolphin, harbour porpoise, pilot whale (blackfish), finback whale, blue whale

Connections and Communications

By air: Regular flights connect Charlottetown to Halifax International Airport and Ottawa, Moncton, Toronto and Boston.

By sea: Ferries connect Borden-Carleton with Cape Tormentine, N.B.; Wood Islands with Caribou, N.S.; Souris with Grindstone, Magdalen Islands, Quebec.

By bridge: The Confederation Bridge opening in 1997 will connect

Cape Bear Lighthouse

Borden-Carleton with Cape Tormentine, N.B., replacing the ferry service.

By road: About 115 km (70 mi.) of the Trans-Canada Highway connect the two ferry terminals of Borden-Carleton and Wood Islands with Charlottetown.

There are 3766 km (2340 mi.) of paved main highways and secondary roads, 864 km (537 mi.) of gravel roads and 662 km (411 mi.) of seasonal roads.

By rail: The last train to the Island ran on July 25, 1990. Passengers travelling to or from P.E.I. on the VIA Rail system take a charter bus between Charlottetown and Summerside and Moncton, N.B.

Newspapers: In Charlottetown, the *Guardian* is published Monday to Saturday; in Summerside, the *Journal Pioneer* is also a daily, and *La Voix Acadienne* is published weekly; in Montague the *Eastern Graphic* is published weekly and *Island Farmer* bi-weekly; in Alberton *The West Prince Graphic* is published weekly and in Souris *The Beacon* is published every second Monday.

TV and radio: There are many television stations available by satellite dish and cable, and three local and regional networks, ATV/ASN (Atlantic Television/Atlantic Satellite Network), CBC TV (Canadian Broadcasting Corporation) and MITV (Maritime Independent Television). There are five radio stations in Charlottetown and two in Summerside, one of which broadcasts in French. Island Cablevision operates out of Summerside and Charlottetown.

Government

Federal: Prince Edward Island has four members in the House of Commons and four in the Senate.

Provincial: There are 27 members of the House of Assembly. Each of the province's 27 electoral districts elects 1 member.

Local: The Island has two cities, 7 towns and 66 communities in its three counties. Cities and towns have a mayor, deputy mayor and administrative councillors. Communities have a chairperson, sometimes a vice-chairperson, and councillors.

Voting qualifications: A person at least 18 years old who has lived in the province for six months and who is either a Canadian citizen or a British subject may vote.

Economy, Industry and Employment

Principal products

Agriculture: Potatoes, dairy produce, cattle, hogs, poultry and eggs. In 1995, farm cash receipts on the Island valued $315.4 million. In 1995, 43 200 ha (108 000 acres) of potatoes were planted.

Fisheries: Lobster, crab, herring, redfish, cod, hake, flounder, mussels, clams, oysters, trout, salmon. Total fish landings were valued at $117 million in 1995, with lobster accounting for $78.4 million.

Tourism: Tourism is one of the Island's three main sources of income. It ranks second, behind agriculture. In 1995, 800 000 tourists spent more than $178 million on P.E.I.

Forestry: There are sawmills, planing mills and millwork industries, on the Island. The total forest production in 1995 was about 684 000 m^3 (896 040 cu.yds.) of wood, 220 000 m^3 (288 200 cu.yds.) of which was fuelwood.

Manufacturing: The value of shipments of goods manufactured in P.E.I. in 1995 was $687.5 million. These goods include transportation equipment, fabricated metal products, chemicals and chemical products, food, fish and wood products.

Employment and income: The provincial and federal governments are the largest employers on the Island. In 1994, 4920 people were employed by the provincial government and about 3150 by the federal government. The value of personal income on Prince Edward Island was about $2378 million in 1994. In 1995, the unemployment rate was 12.3%, the lowest since January 1989.

Education

The degree-granting institutions are the University of Prince Edward Island and the Atlantic Veterinary College, which are on the same Charlottetown campus. A master of science program is offered by U.P.E.I. In 1995, there were 2204 full-time, 477 part-time and 1130 summer students at U.P.E.I.; 197 students at the Vet College; and 25 master of science students.

Holland College provides courses in applied arts and technology, vocational training and adult education. It is divided into three schools and two support divisions, with campuses in Charlottetown and Summerside. In 1995, 4181 (1477 full-time, 2704 part-time) students attended Holland College.

There are 65 public and two private schools, and one band-operated Native school on the Island. In 1995, there were 24 622 students in grades 1-12.

Social and Cultural Life

Museums: There are many historical societies and community museums on the Island. The federal government, through Parks Canada, runs three National Historic Sites, and there are five sites across the Island which are part of the provincial museum system.

Libraries: A library system with 22 branches was established in 1933 when the Carnegie Foundation funded a demonstration project for a rural public library service. The province later assumed responsibility for the system.

The Public Archives of Prince Edward Island was created in 1964. Its holdings include private manuscripts, government and business documents, maps, recordings, photographs, film footage, newspapers, and genealogical records.

Music: Acadian, Scottish and Irish heritage gives Island music its flavour, with year-round concerts and festivals of Scottish and Acadian fiddling, highland dancing and bagpipe playing. In Summerside is the College of Piping and Celtic Performing Arts of Canada.

Don Messer and his Islanders endeared themselves to a generation of Canadians, as has country singer-songwriter Stompin' Tom Connors. Popular, rock-and-roll, jazz, blues and traditional musicians such as Angèle Arsenault, Barachois, Rollo Bay Fiddlers, Chris Corrigan, Chas Guay, Teresa Doyle, Lennie Gallant, Shawn Ferris, Roy Johnstone and many others create a lively music scene. The P.E.I. Symphony performs regularly, offering an annual subscription series.

Sports and Recreation: Outdoor recreation in summer months is plentiful: sailing, fishing, wind surfing, tennis, cycling, horseback riding, golf on 15 courses, swimming, camping in the national park, 13 provincial parks, private campgrounds and trailer parks. A rails-to-trails organization has begun converting torn-up rail beds into hiking and cycling trails.

In winter, favourite sports are hockey, curling, cross-country and downhill skiing.

Harness racing on five tracks is a year-round sport and pastime. Community festivals, ploughing matches, fairs and *ceilidhs* are held throughout the year.

Historic Sites and Landmarks

Ardgowan, in Charlottetown, means "hill of the daisy." It is the restored former residence of William Henry Pope, one of the Fathers of Confederation. The grounds are representative of the garden fashions of the mid-1800s.

Basin Head Fisheries Museum, east of Souris, chronicles the inshore fishing industry in the 18th and 19th centuries through photographs, equipment displays and exhibits. There is a boat shed, fish-canning factory, smoke house and salt-box factory.

Beaconsfield overlooks Charlottetown Harbour. Built in 1877 by James Peake Jr., a wealthy shipping merchant, it is the headquarters of the P.E.I. Museum and Heritage Foundation which publishes *The Island Magazine*.

Confederation Centre of the Arts was opened in 1964 as a national memorial to

the founding of Canada. The Art Gallery and Museum has four galleries, one of which is devoted to the work of Island painter Robert Harris. The complex includes Memorial Hall, an 1100-seat theatre, restaurant, concourses and the Charlottetown Public Library.

Elmira Railway Museum is located east of Souris. This wooden station was the eastern end of the P.E.I. Railway. The museum has displays and exhibits of the Island's railway.

Eptek National Exhibition Centre is located on the waterfront in Summerside. Opened in 1978, the centre has changing exhibits of art, history, science and all aspects of community and national cultural life. The P.E.I. Sports Hall of Fame is located on the site.

Fort Amherst-Port La Joye National Historic Park at Rocky Point, across the harbour from Charlottetown, is the place where the first permanent settlers arrived from France in 1720. An audio-visual presentation gives the history of the site, and visitors can inspect the earthworks of old Fort Amherst.

Green Gables House in the National Park on the north shore at Cavendish is the setting of L.M. Montgomery's famous novel. Visitors can tour the house and explore the nearby "Haunted Wood," "Lovers' Lane" and "Babbling Brook" trails.

Green Park Shipbuilding Museum is in the western part of the province, near Tyne Valley. The Green Park homestead was built in 1865 for shipbuilder James Yeo. In the recreated shipyard are carpenter's and blacksmith's shops, a partially completed sailing vessel and a steam box for bending ship's planking. There is an interpretive centre with photographs and other dislays of the "golden age of sail."

Orwell Corner Historic Village is located 30 km (18 mi.) east of Charlottetown. The farmyard, barns, general store, post office, church, schoolhouse and fields recreate life in the late 1800s. In the summer there are Wednesday night *ceilidhs* where traditional music is played and sung.

Province House National Historic Site at the centre of Charlottetown was the site of the Charlottetown Conference and is still the home of the provincial legislature. It is possible to tour the restored Council chamber, library and other offices.

Sir Andrew Macphail Homestead in Orwell is the gracious home of the author of *The Master's Wife*. There are walking trails throughout the property, on which are stands of old growth hemlock and white pine.

Other Interesting Places to Visit

Acadian Museum of P.E.I. in Miscouche has exhibits that illustrate the way of life and the history of the

Dunvegan Castle is one of more than a dozen large-scale models of famous British castles, churches, inns and homes faithfully reproduced by Lt.-Col. E.W. Johnstone and his son at Woodleigh, near Burlington.

Island's Acadians. Displays include journals, artifacts, photographs, farm tools, textiles and dioramas.

Alberton Museum is in a former courthouse. Its collection includes prehistoric Micmac artifacts, materials from the fox-farming era, costumes, china, toys and other objects of 19th-century life in the Alberton area.

Dalton Centre in Tignish is in a former school named in honour of Sir Charles Dalton, a silver fox breeder. In its two galleries, the history of Tignish and district, and travelling art and historical exhibitions are presented.

Farmers' Bank Museum in South Rustico was built with red Island sandstone in 1863-64. The museum honours the work of Father Georges-Antoine Belcourt, who set up the first client-owned bank in North America.

Garden of the Gulf Museum in Montague is the province's oldest public museum. There are exhibits showing aspects of shipbuilding, local industries, farming and early domestic life, as well as a pictorial history of Montague from 1864 to 1967.

International Fox Hall of Fame and Museum in Summerside preserves the history of the fox fur industry through folk and fine art, photographs, slide and video presentations.

The Keir Memorial Museum is in a former church in Malpeque Village. An exhibit of artifacts and memorabilia depicts life in the nineteenth century.

Lucy Maud Montgomery Birthplace in New London is a small wooden house built in the 1850s. The author's wedding dress and personal scrapbook are on display with other memorabilia.

Micmac Indian Village at Rocky Point illustrates the life of the Micmac before European settlement. A trail through the woods leads past wigwams, a council place, a smoke house and a meat house. A small museum contains a collection of artifacts.

Northumberland Mill and Museum near the village of Murray River is on the site of a once-busy shipyard. There is a working watermill where grain can be ground, and a replica of a turn-of-the-century store.

O'Leary Centennial Museum and adjacent log building and little red schoolhouse display local historical items including medical instruments, an old telephone switchboard and farm implements associated with the early days of potato farming.

Veterans' Memorial Military Museum in Kensington displays a variety of military objects from the Boer War, First and Second World Wars, and the Korean conflict.

West Point Lighthouse Museum is located on the southwest tip of the Island. The story of lighthouses is seen in displays of log books, artifacts and tools.

The Wyatt Centre, endowed by life-long Summerside resident Wanda Wyatt, opened in 1996. The Centre has a 500-seat Harbourfront Jubilee Theatre and is attached to the Eptek Galleries.

Important Dates

1534	Jacques Cartier first sights P.E.I.
1720	250 French settlers arrive
1731	Jean-Pierre Roma settles in Trois Rivières
1755	Mainland Acadians who escaped deportation arrive on the Island
1758	The British win the Island from France, establish Fort Amherst and deport most of the Island Acadians
1763	Britain gains control of North America. Île St-Jean becomes St. John's Island and is annexed to Nova Scotia
1764-65	Samuel Holland surveys the Island, divides it into three counties and 67 lots, and names Charlottetown as its capital
1767	Great lottery held in London, in which most of the Island's 67 lots are raffled off
1769	The Island is separated from Nova Scotia; Walter Patterson becomes its first governor
1770	Scottish settlers arrive at Stanhope and Malpeque
1771	First record of potato-growing on the Island
1772	The Glenaladale settlers arrive from Scotland with Captain John MacDonald
1773	First elections held on the Island
1775	Charlottetown is raided by American privateers
1799	The Island is renamed in honour of Prince Edward, the Duke of Kent

1803	The Selkirk settlers arrive
1815	Large numbers of immigrants from Ireland begin to arrive
1827	Iceboats begin regular winter mail service across the Northumberland Strait
1830	Roman Catholics are given the vote
1841	824 settlers from Ireland arrive on the Island
1851	The Island is granted responsible government
1852	The first underwater telegraph cable in North America is laid between New Brunswick and the Island
1855	Charlottetown is incorporated as a city
1864	The Charlottetown Conference is held to discuss the idea of Confederation
1867	Nova Scotia, New Brunswick, Ontario and Quebec unite as the Dominion of Canada
1870	Lennox Island is purchased for the Micmac
1873	Prince Edward Island joins Confederation
1875	The Land Purchase Act is passed
1877	The town of Summerside is incorporated
1884	The tricolour flag is adoped by Maritime Acadians at the Miscouche Conference
1886	The first harness race event is held in Summerside
1887	The first electric lights are lit on the Island
1894	The first silver fox is bred in captivity by Robert Oulton and Charles Dalton
1905	A bridge is erected over the Hillsborough River
1908	L.M. Montgomery's *Anne of Green Gables* is published
1916	Rail-ferry service to the mainland begins
1918	First seed potatoes produced in Canada are shipped from P.E.I.
1922	Island women win the right to vote in provincial elections
1934	The first road is paved on the Island
1941	Canadian Forces Base (CFB) Summerside opens
1964	Confederation Centre of the Arts opens in Charlottetown
1969	The University of Prince Edward Island is formed
1972	The Abegweit Band of Island Micmac is formed
1973	A causeway to Lennox Island is completed
1986	The first annual National Milton Acorn Festival is held in Charlottetown in honour of the Island-born poet
1988	The government holds a plebiscite on the fixed link
1989	CFB Summerside is shut down
1990	The last train runs on the Island railway
1992	Canada's first ministers and territorial and Native leaders meet in Charlottetown and agree on a constitutional reform package known as the Charlottetown Accord; the Accord is later rejected in a national referendum
1997	Confederation Bridge linking P.E.I. with New Brunswick opens

Important People

Milton Acorn (1923-1986), born at Charlottetown; poet; honoured in 1970 by leading Canadian writers as "The People's Poet of Canada;" received the Governor General's Award for Poetry in 1975 for *The Island Means Minago*. There is a National Milton Acorn Festival on the Island in his honour every summer

Georges Arsenault (1952-), born in Abram-Village; professor of Acadian studies at U.P.E.I.; cultural co-ordinator of St. Thomas Aquinas Society; writer and broadcaster. Arsenault's book *The Island Acadians* won the 1988 Prix France-Acadie

Iphigenie Arsenault (1908-), born in Summerside; employed with P.E.I. Division of the Canadian Red Cross Society for over 50 years; held top administrative position from 1944 to 1978; received Queen's Jubilee Medal and Order of Canada

Leone Bagnall (1933-), born in Springfield; educator; member of the Legislative Assembly; former minister of education and minister responsible for status of women; acting leader of the opposition, 1992

Rev. Georges-Antoine Belcourt (1803-1874), Roman Catholic priest; after 27 years of missionary work in the West, came to the Island where he founded the Farmers' Bank of South Rustico, the forerunner of the credit union movement

Rev. Francis Bolger (1925-), born in Stanley Bridge; author of six books on Prince Edward Island and L.M. Montgomery; enthusiastic Island history professor at St. Dunstan's University and at U.P.E.I.

Carl Frederick Burke (1913-1976), born in Charlottetown; pilot, entrepreneur; flew during the Second World War, and afterward started his own air service, Maritime Central Airways, which became Canada's largest independent cargo airline

Catherine S. Callbeck (1939-), born in Summerside; business-woman, politician; premier from 1993-96; the first woman in Canada to be elected premier

Alex B. Campbell (1933-), born in Summerside; lawyer, politician; premier of the province from 1966 to 1978; appointed Justice of Supreme Court of Prince Edward Island

Stompin' Tom Connors (1937-), singer-songwriter; adopted at age 7 by a family from Skinner's Pond; wrote his first song when he was 11 years old and has by now written more than 500, mainly chronicling the lives of

Iphigenie Arsenault

Leone Bagnall

Catherine Callbeck

Stompin' Tom Connors

Evelyn Cudmore

Elizabeth Epperly

Joseph A. Ghiz

George Godfrey

working people and small towns of Canada; nicknamed for his habit of stomping with his left foot to keep time

William Cooper (c. 1786-1862), born in England; sea captain, farmer, shipbuilder, merchant, politician; also a land agent, he switched loyalties to become a supporter of tenants and to lead a land reform movement

Evelyn MacEwen Cudmore (1909-1992), born in Bristol; volunteer worker who had a major impact on Island society; was associated with the Red Cross for nearly 50 years, promoting the health and safety of Islanders

Dr. Elizabeth Rollins Epperly (1951-   ), born in Virginia; writer, English professor; lifelong L.M. Montgomery enthusiast and eminent Montgomery scholar; appointed president of the University of Prince Edward Island in 1995

Joseph A. Ghiz (1945-1996), born in Charlottetown; lawyer, politician; premier from 1986-1992; Dean of Law at Dalhousie University 1993-95; named P.E.I. Supreme Court justice in 1995

George Godfrey (1852-1901), born in Charlottetown; boxer; American Black Heavyweight Champion and one of top heavyweight fighters in the world in the 1880s

Reshard Gool (1931-1989), professor, writer, editor; founder of Square Deal Press; co-founder with his wife, graphic artist **Hilda Woolnough**, of the Gallery on Demand, where many Island writers and artists gathered. Gool and Woolnough received the first Prince Edward Island Council of the Arts Award for Outstanding Contribution to the Literary Arts

Michel Haché-Gallant (c.1663-1737), probably the first Acadian to settle on the Island; part Micmac, possibly the son of Pierre Larche, a Frenchman, and his Micmac wife; was port captain of Port LaJoye and is buried there

Robert Harris (1849-1919), born in Wales, emigrated with his family to P.E.I. at the age of 7; painter; president of the Royal Canadian Academy; known for his portraits and for works such as *A Meeting of the School Trustees* and *The Fathers of Confederation*

Sarah Harvie (1832-1907), born in Charlottetown; educator; from 1848 to 1903, taught more than 2000 students at the Bog School, where most of Charlottetown's Blacks lived. Her conscientious work made the school a great success over her 56 years of service

Geoff Hogan (1953-1992), born in Charlottetown; biologist, educator, writer; his knowledge and love of birds and bird habitats contributed greatly to making Islanders more informed and concerned about their natural environment

Samuel Johannes Holland (1728-1801), born in Holland; surveyor, cartographer, military engineer; joined the British army in 1754 and took part in the sieges of Louisbourg and Quebec; directed the survey of the Island in 1764

Robert T. Holman (1833-1906), merchant, shipbuilder and owner; opened a small store in Summerside in 1856 and eventually owned the largest department store on the Island, a meat and poultry cannery and a lobster factory

Elsie Inman (1890-1986), born in West River; suffragist; appeared before the legislature alone in 1920 to battle for women's right to vote; appointed Senator; helped organize the Liberal Women of P.E.I.

M. Elizabeth (Betty) Large (1913-1990), radio personality; worked in broadcasting from the age of 12 when she read bedtime stories over her father's experimental radio station; co-founder with her husband, **R.F. Large,** of the Island's first TV station and part of its management for many years; wrote a history of Island broadcasting, *Out of Thin Air*

Eleanor M. Lowe (1908-), born in Charlottetown; taught art at

Prince of Wales College for more than 40 years; was active in the Art Society and promoted art education

Donald McDonald (1783-1867), evangelist; settled on the Island in 1826; considered himself "the Trumpet of the Lord" and was famous for his preaching; built more than a dozen churches and wrote words to many hymns which are still sung today

Angus Bernard MacEachern (1759-1835), born in Scotland, came to P.E.I. in 1790; considered the father of Roman Catholicism on the Island; appointed Bishop in 1829, was responsible for obtaining vote for Roman Catholics

J. Angus MacLean (1914-), born in Lewes; politician; Member of Parliament 1951-76; federal fisheries minister 1957-63; Conservative premier of P.E.I. from 1979 to 1981; received the Order of Canada in 1992

Sir Andrew Macphail (1864-1938), born in Orwell; physician, man of letters, professor; published ten books and many articles on social and political topics; his semi-autobiographical book, *The Master's Wife*, provides insight into 19th-century Island life

Lucy Maud Montgomery (1874-1942), born in Clifton; writer. Although her first novel, *Anne of Green Gables*, was rejected many times before it was accepted, it

Geoff Hogan

Robert T. Holman

Elsie Inman

L.M. Montgomery

Joe O'Brien

Libby Zoë Oughton

Marion L. Reid

Michael Thomas

became an instant best seller after it was published in 1908. Since then her novels and short stories have influenced the lives of millions of readers around the world

Joe O'Brien (1917-1984), born in Alberton; driver and trainer of harness horses; set world's pacing record and drove more sub-two-minute miles than any other harness driver in history; considered one of the world's best

Libby Zoë Oughton (1938-), poet, publisher and artist; owner of Ragweed Press 1980-1989 and ardent supporter and promoter of Island writers; began an imprint for women writers and produced a grade 6 social studies textbook; received the Award for Outstanding Contribution to the Arts in 1992

Walter Patterson (c. 1735-1798), born in Ireland; army officer, land speculator, colonial administrator; became the first governor of St. John's Island and served for 17 years

Georgina Pope (1862-1938), born in Summerside; first matron of the Canadian Army Medical Corps; led the group of nurses who served in South Africa during the Boer War; the first Canadian to receive the Royal Red Cross for conspicuous service in the field

William Henry Pope (1825-1879), born at Bedeque; politician; appointed colonial secretary of the Island in 1859; an advocate of Confederation, he was a delegate to the Charlottetown and Quebec conferences

Henry Purdy (1937-), visual artist; director of Holland College School of Visual Arts, later the School of Creative Arts; appointed to Canada Council 1984-1991

Marion L. Reid (1929-), born in North Rustico; educator, former speaker of the Legislature; Lieutenant-Governor of P.E.I. from 1990-1995, the first woman to hold the position

Irene Rogers (1921-1991), born in Norboro; historian and writer whose keen interest in the preservation of the Island's heritage kept many buildings from being torn down

Michael Thomas (1883-1954), born on Lennox Island; member of Lennox Island Micmac Band; the Island's best and one of Canada's top long-distance runners

Moncrieff Williamson (1915-), poet, novelist; first director of the Confederation Centre Art Gallery and Museum from 1964 to 1982; biographer of painter Robert Harris

Mona Wilson (1894-1981), pioneer in public health in P.E.I; directed the public health nursing service for 30 years and was chief Red Cross nurse from 1923 to 1931

James Yeo (1789-1868), lumber dealer; storekeeper; justice of the peace; businessman; the largest shipbuilder on the Island, he was the richest man on the Island when he died

Mona Wilson

Premiers of Prince Edward Island Since Confederation

James C. Pope	Conservative	1873
Lemuel C. Owen	Conservative	1873-76
Louis H. Davies	Coalition	1876-79
William W. Sullivan	Conservative	1879-89
Neil McLeod	Conservative	1889-91
Frederick Peters	Liberal	1891-97
Alexander B. Warburton	Liberal	1897-98
Donald Farquharson	Liberal	1898-1901
Arthur Peters	Liberal	1901-08
Francis L. Haszard	Liberal	1908-11
H. James Palmer	Liberal	1911
John A. Mathieson	Conservative	1911-17
Aubin E. Arsenault	Conservative	1917-19
John H. Bell	Liberal	1919-23
James D. Stewart	Conservative	1923-27
Albert C. Saunders	Liberal	1927-30
Walter M. Lea	Liberal	1930-31
James D. Stewart	Conservative	1931-33
William J.P. MacMillan	Conservative	1933-35
Walter M. Lea	Liberal	1935-36
Thame A. Campbell	Liberal	1936-43
J. Walter Jones	Liberal	1943-53
Alexander W. Matheson	Liberal	1953-59
Walter R. Shaw	Conservative	1959-66
Alexander B. Campbell	Liberal	1966-78
W. Bennett Campbell	Liberal	1978-79
J. Angus MacLean	Conservative	1979-81
James M. Lee	Conservative	1981-86
Joseph A. Ghiz	Liberal	1986-92
Catherine S. Callbeck	Liberal	1993-96
Keith Milligan	Liberal	1996
Patrick G. Binns	Conservative	1996-

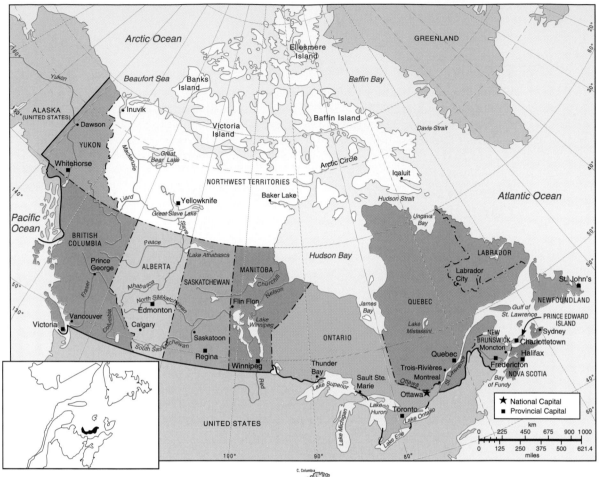

Arctic Ocean

GREENLAND

Ellesmere
Island

Beaufort Sea

Banks
Island

Baffin Bay

ALASKA
(UNITED STATES)

• Inuvik

Victoria
Island

Baffin Island

Davis Strait

• Dawson

YUKON

Great
Bear Lake

Arctic Circle

• Whitehorse

Iqaluit

Pacific
Ocean

NORTHWEST TERRITORIES

Atlantic Ocean

Yellowknife

Baker Lake

Hudson Strait

Great Slave Lake

BRITISH
COLUMBIA

Peace

Ungava
Bay

LABRADOR

Lake Athabasca

• Prince
George

ALBERTA

MANITOBA

SASKATCHEWAN

Hudson Bay

Labrador
City

Athabasca

Churchill

Flin Flon

Nelson

QUEBEC

St. John's

NEWFOUNDLAND

• Edmonton

North Saskatchewan

James
Bay

Lake
Mistassini

PRINCE EDWARD
ISLAND

Victoria

Vancouver

• Calgary

Saskatoon

Lake
Winnipeg

ONTARIO

Gulf of
St. Lawrence

NEW
BRUNSWICK

Sydney

Charlottetown

South Saskatchewan

Regina

Winnipeg

Thunder
Bay

Trois-Rivières
Quebec

Moncton

Halifax

Fredericton

Montreal

NOVA SCOTIA

Red

Sault Ste.
Marie

Ottawa

Bay
of Fundy

Lake Superior

★ National Capital
■ Provincial Capital

Lake Michigan

Lake
Huron

Toronto

Lake Ontario

UNITED STATES

Lake Erie

km
0 225 450 675 900 1000

0 125 250 375 500 621.4
miles

© Hammond Inc., Maplewood, N.J.

Topography

QUEEN ELIZABETH ISLANDS

Ellesmere
Island

Beaufort
Sea

Banks

Victoria
Island

Baffin
Bay

Baffin
Island

Mt. Logan
19,524 ft.
(5951 m.)

Mt.
Fairweather
15,300 ft.
(4663 m.)

Great
Slave Lake

Foxe
Basin

Hudson
Bay

QUEEN
CHARLOTTE IS.

Peace

Ungava
Peninsula

Ungava
Bay

Newfoundland

Vancouver
I.

Athabasca

Reindeer

PLATEAU

Gulf of
St. Lawrence

Cape Breton
I.

Edmonton

Nelson

Saskatchewan

Nova
Scotia

Sable I.

Regina

Winnipeg

Lake
Mistassini

Manitoba

L. of
the Woods

L.
Nipigon

Lake
Superior

Ottawa

Montréal

Québec

Winnipeg

Toronto

L. Ontario

Manitoulin I.

Georgian
Bay

L.
Huron

Niagara
Falls

Halifax

5,000 m. 2,000 m. 1,000 m. 500 m. 200 m. 100 m. Sea
16,404 ft. 6,562 ft. 3,281 ft. 1,640 ft. 656 ft. 328 ft. Level
Below

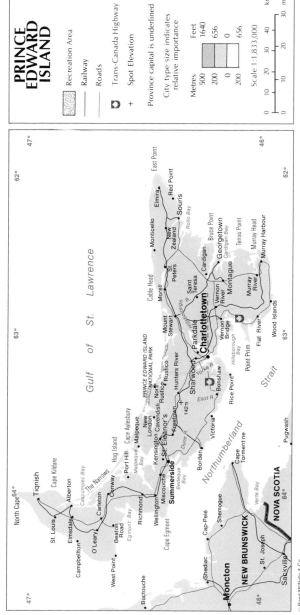

PRINCE EDWARD ISLAND

Recreation Area

— Railway

— Roads

⊡ Trans-Canada Highway

+ Spot Elevation

⊡ Province capital is underlined

City type size indicates
relative importance

Metres	Feet
500	1640
200	656
0	0
200	656

Scale 1:1,833,000

km	0	10	20	30	40	
	0	10	20	30		mi

© Rand McNally & Co.
A-520207-772

Gulf of St. Lawrence

North Cape 64°
Tiqnish
Cape Kildare
Elmsdale
Alberton
St. Louis
Campbellton
O'Leary
Beaton Road
West Point
Carleton
Conway
The Narrows
Hog Island
Port Hill
Cape Aylesbury
Malpeque
Malpeque Bay
Cascumpec Bay
Egmont Bay
Cape Egmont
Richmond
Miscouche
Wellington
Summerside
Bedeque Bay
New London
Kensington
North Rustico
Rustico
PRINCE EDWARD ISLAND
NATIONAL PARK
New
London
Cavendish
St. Eleanor's
Dunk R.
Borden
Victoria
Bonshaw
Sherwood
Hunters River
142m +
Eliot R.
York R.
Mount
Stewart
Parkdale
Charlottetown
Morell
Cable Head
St. Peters
Saint Teresa
Cardigan
Georgetown
Cardigan Bay
Bruce Point
New
Zealand
Monticello
Elmira
East Point
Red Point
Souris
Rollo Bay
Vernon
River
Vernon
Bridge
Montague
Murray
River
Terras Point
Murray Head
Murray Harbour
Flat River
Wood Islands
Point Prim
Rice Point
Hillsborough Bay
Northumberland Strait

Cape
Torment ne
Shemogue
Cap-Pelé
Verte Bay
Pugwash
NOVA SCOTIA

Shediac
Moncton
Buctouche
NEW BRUNSWICK
St. Joseph
Sackville
46°

47° North Cape 64°

47° 63° 62° 47°

46° 64° 63° 62° 46°

AVERAGE ANNUAL RAINFALL

The central part of Prince Edward Island receives the greatest amount of rain.

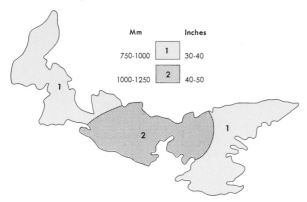

Mm		Inches
750-1000	1	30-40
1000-1250	2	40-50

Figures within areas are for identification purposes only.

GROWING SEASON

Most of Prince Edward Island has about five frost-free months each year.

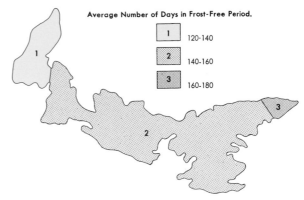

Average Number of Days in Frost-Free Period.

1	120-140
2	140-160
3	160-180

Figures within areas are for identification purposes only.

ECONOMY AND AGRICULTURE

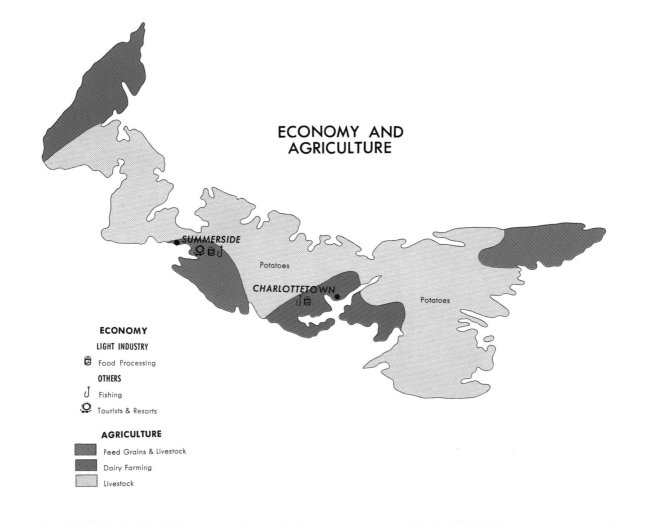

SUMMERSIDE

Potatoes

CHARLOTTETOWN

Potatoes

ECONOMY

LIGHT INDUSTRY

Food Processing

OTHERS

Fishing

Tourists & Resorts

AGRICULTURE

Feed Grains & Livestock

Dairy Farming

Livestock

Index

127

About the Author

Deirdre Kessler is the author of a dozen books for young adults and children. Her series of novels about a character named Brupp has an international audience. Ms. Kessler has toured widely in the United States, Canada, the Netherlands and Germany. She has been a teacher in elementary, junior high, high school and university, a radio and television writer and a performer. Ms. Kessler lives in Charlottetown, Prince Edward Island, where she is currently a freelance writer and broadcaster.